PAPER
CRAFT

PAPER CRAFT

Senior Art Editor Gemma Fletcher
Project Editor James Mitchem
Additional design Charlotte Bull, Stefan Georgiou,
Samantha Richiardi, Sadie Thomas
US Editors Christy Lusiak, Shannon Beatty
Additional Editing Anne Hildyard,
Toby Mann, Kate Meeker
Art Direction for Photography Sonia Moore
Photographer Dave King
Consultant Jennifer Wendell Kosek
Managing Editor Penny Smith
Managing Art Editor Marianne Markham
Senior Jacket Creative Nicola Powling
Jacket Design Assistant Amy Keast
Jacket Coordinator Francesca Young
Jacket Quiller Yulia Brodskaya
Senior Producer, Pre-production Tony Phipps
Senior Producer Ché Creasey
Creative Technical Support Sonia Charbonnier
Creative Director Jane Bull
Category Publisher Mary Ling

First American Edition, 2015
Published in the United States by DK Publishing
345 Hudson Street, New York, New York 10014

Copyright © 2015 Dorling Kindersley Limited
DK, a Division of Penguin Random House LLC

15 16 17 18 19 10 9 8 7 6 5 4 3 2 1
001–280245–October/2015

Published in Great Britain by
Dorling Kindersley Limited.

A catalog record for this book is available from the
Library of Congress.
ISBN: 978-1-4654-3943-7

DK books are available at special discounts when purchased in
bulk for sales promotions, premiums, fund-raising, or educational
use. For details, contact: DK Publishing Special Markets, 345 Hudson
Street, New York, New York 10014 SpecialSales@dk.com

Printed and bound in China

All images © Dorling Kindersley Limited
For further information see: www.dkimages.com

A WORLD OF IDEAS:
SEE ALL THERE IS TO KNOW
www.dk.com

Contents

Introduction 6
Basic equipment 8
Types of paper 10

Cards and gift wrap 12
Pop-up bouquet 14
Feather gift tag 20
DIY envelopes 24
Mini gift box 28
Quilling 32
Gift box 36
Pyramid gift box 42
Customized paper 44
3D star tag 46

Gifts to give 48
Layered papercut 50
Quilled earrings 56
Nursery papercut 60
Papercut locket 64
Papercut lantern 66
Silhouette frame 72

Decorations 76
Honeycomb pom-pom 78
Origami fairy lights 84
Hanging fan 88
Hanging garlands 94
Snowflake ornament 98

Kids' crafts 102
Origami bird 104
Animal mask 108
Owl mobile 112
Party crown 118

Flowers 122
Cherry blossom 124
Peony 128
Ranunculus 132
Daisy 136
Anemone 140
Daffodil 144
Large rose 148
Kusudama 152
Wreath 156
Boutonniere 160
Large poppy 164
Festival headband 170

Scrapbooking 174
Making a scrapbook 176
Photo corners and frames 176
Bunting and bows 180
Storage pockets 182
Rosettes 184
Gilding and embossing 186
Travel 188
Wedding 190
Baby's first year 192
Scrapbooking templates 194

Templates 196

Index 220

Acknowledgments 222

Introduction

Ever since paper was invented in China more than 2,000 years ago, it has been used to create beautiful objects—from books, maps, and paintings to flowers and origami. Paper has become one of the most versatile crafting materials known to humans, and this book will show you how to use it to create beautiful, personalized craft projects.

For each project we've included a list of the materials you will need, and also supplied templates when called for. We hope you enjoy the book, and that it provides you with the skills and inspiration to make beautiful paper objects you can call your own.

Basic equipment

One of the great things about making crafts from paper is you don't need lots of expensive equipment. We'll list everything you'll need for each project individually, but the basics covered on this page are used regularly throughout the book, so they are a good investment.

Ruler

Scissors

Cutting mat

Circle punch

Small scissors

Pliers

Craft knife

Utility knife

Hole punch

Assortment of tapes

Spray mount

Hot glue gun

PVA glue

Hot glue stick

Glue dots

Sticky tack

Glue stick

Scorer

Watercolor paints

Pens

Colored pencils

Pencil

Eraser

Bone folder

Brushes

Types of paper

Flexible and relatively inexpensive, paper is a fantastic and versatile material for craft projects. Here's an overview of the different types that you'll need, and a few details to keep in mind.

Paper types
Unless otherwise stated, the projects can all be made with standard paper or one of those listed on the opposite page.

Weight
The greater a paper's weight, the thicker and stronger it will be. Generally speaking, this will be reflected in the cost.

Style
One of the best qualities of paper is its variety. The number of different patterns and designs available is almost endless.

Color
Don't feel like you have to stick to the colors used in the book. Be sure to experiment and make the projects personal to you.

Tracing paper
Transparent paper used for copying images, tracing paper is used to transfer the templates onto your desired paper or cardstock.

Crepe paper
A thin, pliable paper perfect for making flowers. If you want to make it stronger, stick two sheets together with spray mount.

Quilling paper
Thin strips of paper that are twisted into different shapes. They're available in a great number of styles and colors.

Tissue paper
A very thin, lightweight paper. In addition to being useful for craft projects, it's the perfect material for lining gift boxes.

Origami paper
Usually only one side of origami paper is colored, but this isn't always the case. The only rules are that it's square and folds well.

Cardstock
Cardstock is a heavier weight than standard paper and is available in various colors and finishes.

Cards and gift wrap

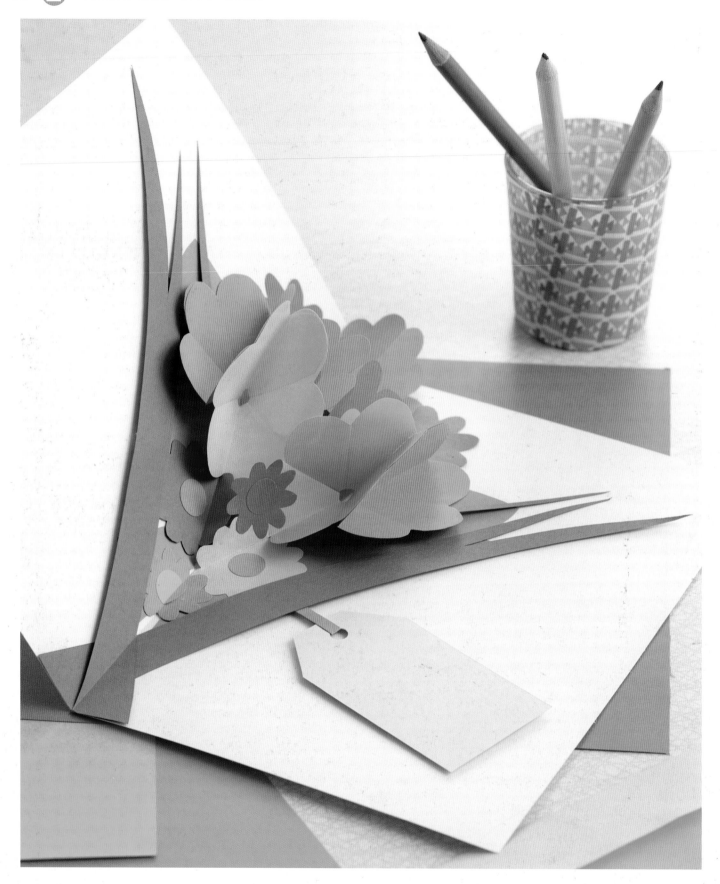

Pop-up bouquet

This cheerful and personal card will bring a smile to anyone's face. It's ideal to send to someone special on a birthday or anniversary, and it works well as a get well soon or congratulations card.

Cutting mat

Tracing paper

Colored cardstock

Scorer

Pencil

Scissors

Double-sided tape

Ruler

You will need

White cardstock, folded in half

Trace all the pieces of the template and position them image side down on the colored cardstock. Rub over the pattern with a pencil to transfer the image onto the cardstock.

Carefully score along any dotted lines and cut out any solid lines with scissors or a craft knife. Repeat this until you've cut and scored all the pieces of the template.

The four central flowers that need to be assembled are made in pairs. Fold along the score marks and overlap the first and seventh petals to make a cone shape, using tape to secure. Fold in half as shown on the orange flower.

You will need two sets of these flowers.

Stick double-sided tape to two petals and attach a different colored flower, leaving one petal unattached at either end. You should end up with a shape that is four petals wide and only attached at the middle two petals.

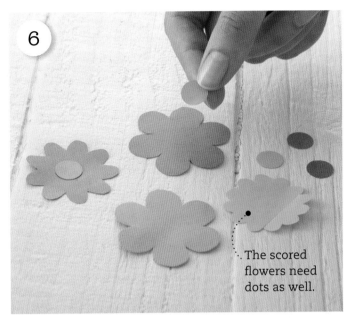

Fold the small pink central flower that is scored in three places and stick one side on the card at the angle pictured above. Peel the backing off the tape on the top edge and fold the card in half so the other half sticks in the right position.

Using the double-sided tape or a little glue, stick a dot in the middle of the central flower so it sits on either side of the fold. Then stick colored dots in the middle of all the remaining flowers.

The scored flowers need dots as well.

Align with the gutter.

Fold and position one side of the green leaf as shown. It's crucial that the point of the crease is in the gutter and the top edge is 1½in (4cm) from the gutter. Apply tape to the top and close the card so the other side sticks in the correct spot.

Stick the two flowers that have nine petals in position on either side of the central folded flower. Then stick the two large flowers that have six petals to the top edge of the green leaf—one on either side.

Add a small blade of grass to the back of two of the central flowers that you assembled in steps 3 and 4.

Stick the grass on this petal

Position the central flowers into the crease in the middle as shown. There should only be tape on the bottom petal.

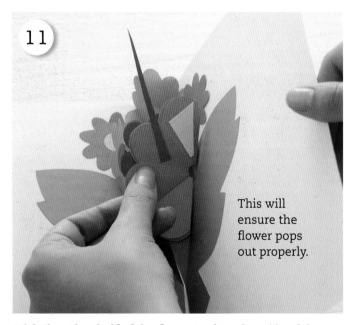

This will ensure the flower pops out properly.

Stick the other half of the flower to the other side of the card, but this time add tape to just the top petal. Stick on the remaining central flowers in the same way.

Stick the two medium-sized flowers with score lines on either side of the fold. Then add the little red flower above them, and the little pink one below.

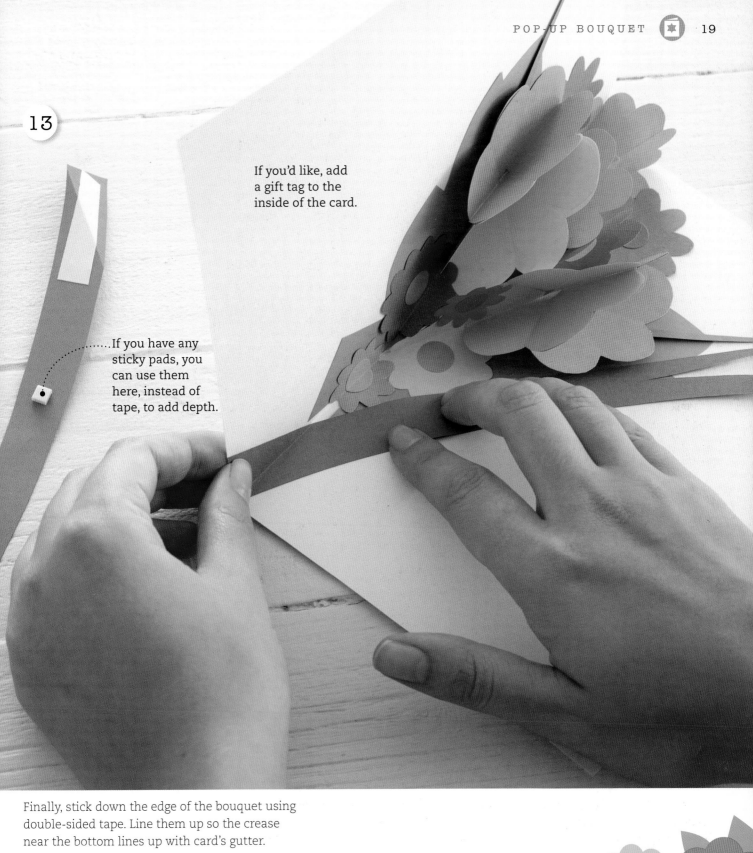

13

If you'd like, add a gift tag to the inside of the card.

......If you have any sticky pads, you can use them here, instead of tape, to add depth.

Finally, stick down the edge of the bouquet using double-sided tape. Line them up so the crease near the bottom lines up with card's gutter.

Feather gift tag

Not only are these simple feather tags the perfect way to elevate your gifts, they also make great little decorations or place cards for a dinner party.

Selection of cardstock

Scissors

Pencil

Scorer

Tracing paper

You will need

1

Trace the templates and lay them face down on cardstock. Rub to transfer.

2

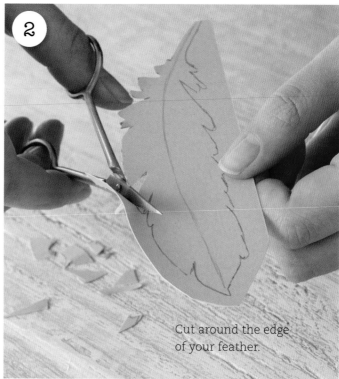

Cut around the edge of your feather.

3

Score along the middle of the feather then pinch to bend along the scored line.

4

Cut slices toward the middle to create a feathery effect.

Tie ribbon around the bottom and attach to gifts.

DIY envelopes

These little envelopes are the perfect complement to handmade cards, and can be sealed with a sticker, glue, or wax. Best of all, with a little practice, they can be made in a flash.

You will need

Squares of paper

Ruler

Pencil

Eraser

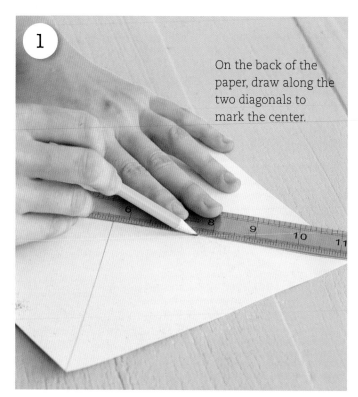

1 On the back of the paper, draw along the two diagonals to mark the center.

2 Fold two opposite corners into the center, then fold and unfold a third corner.

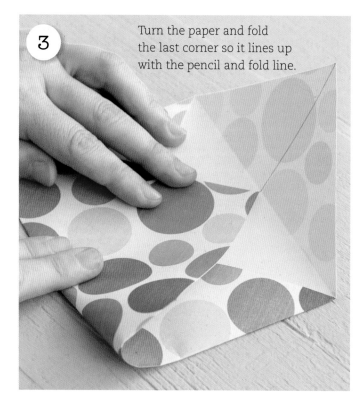

3 Turn the paper and fold the last corner so it lines up with the pencil and fold line.

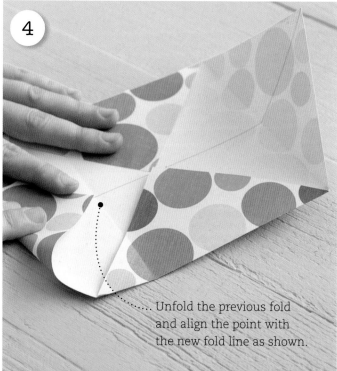

4 Unfold the previous fold and align the point with the new fold line as shown.

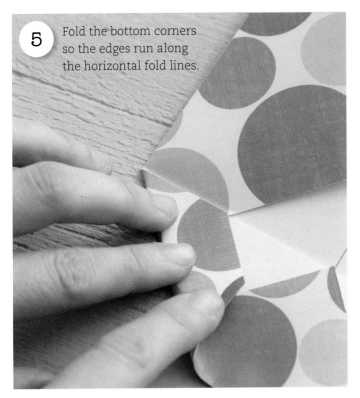

5 Fold the bottom corners so the edges run along the horizontal fold lines.

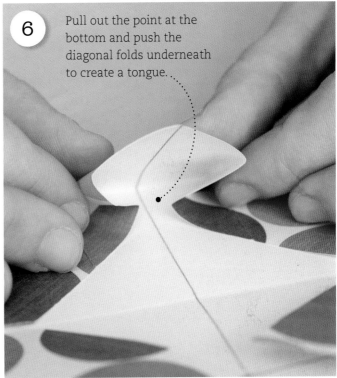

6 Pull out the point at the bottom and push the diagonal folds underneath to create a tongue.

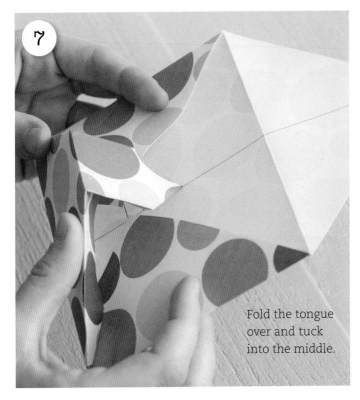

7 Fold the tongue over and tuck into the middle.

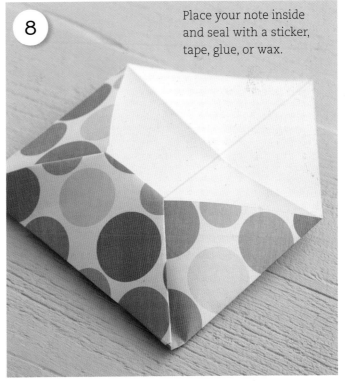

8 Place your note inside and seal with a sticker, tape, glue, or wax.

Mini gift box

This little box is easy to make and provides a fun, sturdy wrapping solution for all kinds of small gifts. Experiment with different paper colors and weights that will suit your gift.

You will need

Bone folder

Square cardstock or heavy paper

1 Fold the paper in half twice to make a square, then open it back out.

Fold diagonally, then open and fold along the other diagonal.

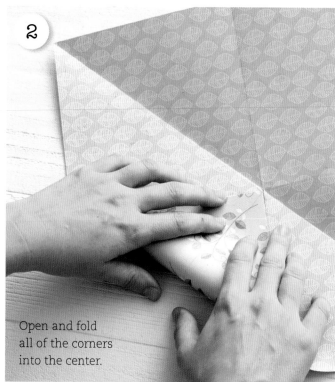

2 Open and fold all of the corners into the center.

3 Fold two of the edges inward so they meet in the middle. Unfold and repeat with the other sides.

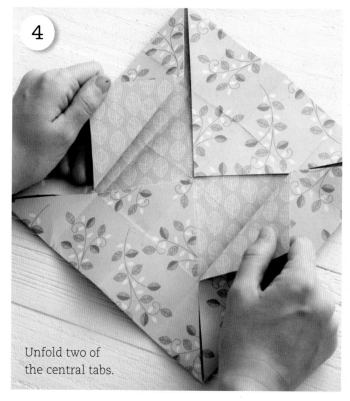

4 Unfold two of the central tabs.

5 Turn the box and lift up the sides.

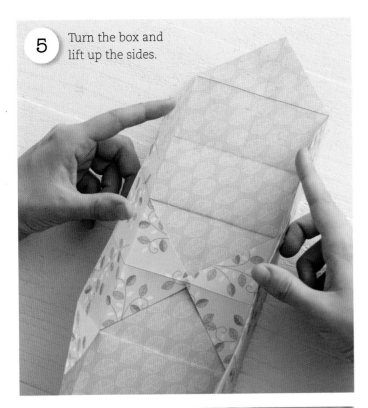

6 Fold the sides in as shown, then fold the top point into the center of the box.

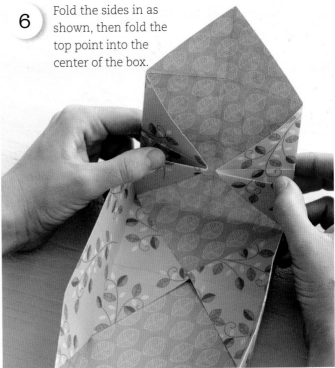

7 Turn the box on its side and push into all of the corners to secure.

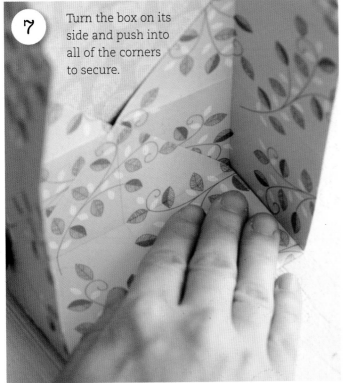

8 Repeat on the other side, then make the other half of the box.

Use slightly smaller paper for the other half of the box.

Quilling

Quilling is easier than it looks, even if it seems intimidating at first.
Once you can make the basic shapes, it's just a matter of gluing them
in place on the card to make interesting patterns.

Quilling paper

Brush

PVA glue

Quilling tool

Cardstock

You will need

Tight coil   Loose coil   Open coil   Marquise   Teardrop

Coiling

To make a coil, place your paper into the quilling tool so no paper emerges from the other side. Wind the paper around the tool, using your finger to ensure the coil is flat. You can make different shapes by adjusting how tight the coil is.

Gluing

Be quite sparing with the glue.

Use a small brush or toothpick to add glue to keep a coil's shape. If you want to make a loose coil, allow the paper to unravel before applying the glue. For an open coil, let it unravel and don't apply any glue at all.

S Scroll　　　　　　　　　　　Heart　　　　　　　　　　　V Scroll

Shaping

Most quilled shapes are created by making adjustments to the basic coils. For example, to make a marquise, you simply create a loose coil and pinch it on both ends. To make a teardrop, you do the same, but only pinch one end.

Experimenting

Experiment to create the other shapes. For example, a heart is made by folding a strip of paper in half and winding each end toward the center, and a V scroll is made by doing the same but winding it away from the center.

Gift box

If you're planning on giving somebody a small gift, these little boxes are an excellent way to present them. Simply line them with tissue paper and fill with treats. They also work well for favors.

Ribbon

Craft knife

Scorer

Ruler

Scrap surface

Tracing paper

Hole punch

Bone folder

Brush

Pencil

PVA Glue

Cutting mat

Paper

You will need

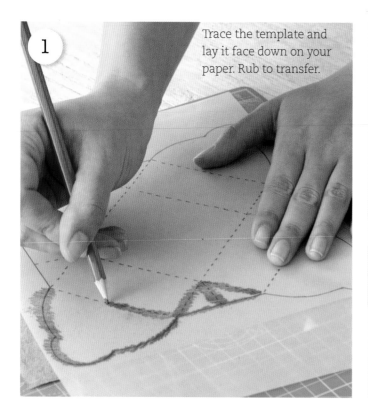

1 Trace the template and lay it face down on your paper. Rub to transfer.

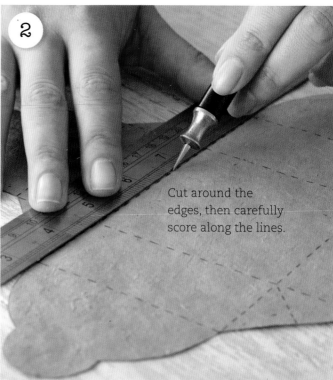

2 Cut around the edges, then carefully score along the lines.

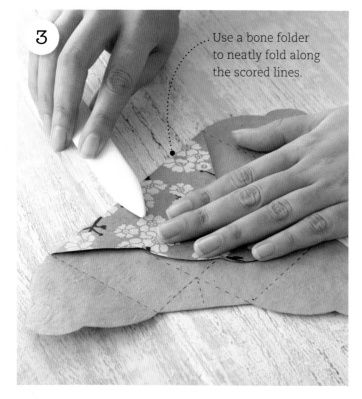

3 Use a bone folder to neatly fold along the scored lines.

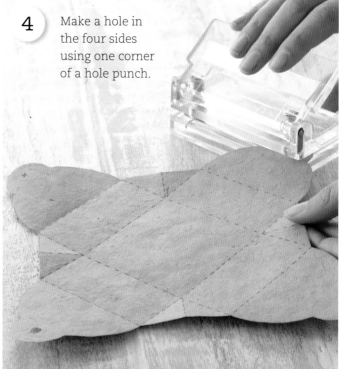

4 Make a hole in the four sides using one corner of a hole punch.

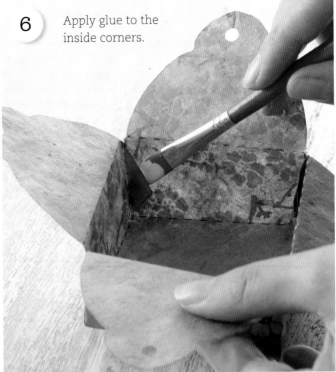

5 Fold the box inward, then apply glue to the corner folds as shown.

6 Apply glue to the inside corners.

7 Thread a strand of ribbon through the holes to finish.

Use the alternative templates to create a range of boxes that suit different types of gifts.

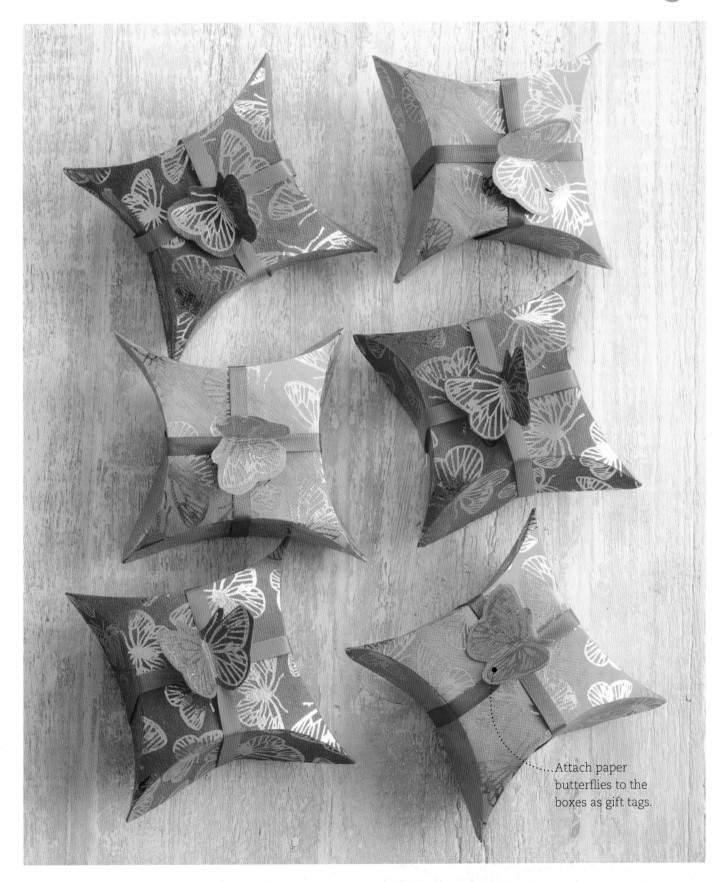

Attach paper butterflies to the boxes as gift tags.

Pyramid gift box

An alternative gift box design, this pyramid version is ideal for giving small gifts such as jewelry. They're easy to make and, as an added bonus, they are entirely reusable.

You will need

···· Strong paper

String
or ribbon ········

PVA glue
and brush

1 Transfer the template to paper and fold along the scored lines. Punch out the holes and glue the edges as shown.

2

Fill the boxes, then thread string through the four holes and tie in a bow to seal.

Customized paper

There's no better way to make wrapping paper, envelopes, and gift boxes unique than by creating customized paper. Here's a quick and simple way to make your own.

You will need

- Pencil
- Craft knife
- Scorer
- Ink pad
- Selection of paper
- Eraser

Draw your design onto an eraser. It can be anything you like, but try not to make it too detailed or it'll be hard to cut.

Being very careful, cut around the outside of your design. You want to cut only about halfway through the eraser.

Using a scorer, make shallow indentations to the detailed areas of the design.

Press your stamp onto an ink pad, then press onto the paper. Experiment with the position to create different patterns.

3D star tag

These little star tags are a great way to make your gifts out of this world. They're simple to make, so prepare a big batch and give them to the "stars" in your life when needed.

You will need

- Tracing paper
- Pencil
- Paper or cardstock
- Craft knife
- Ruler
- Scorer

1

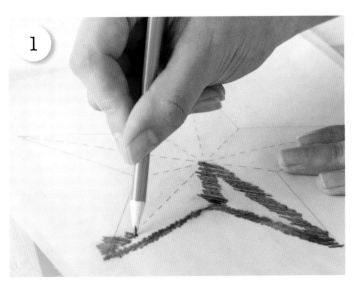

Trace the templates and lay them face down on the paper or card. Rub with a pencil to transfer the image.

2

Carefully cut around the outside of the star design. Use a ruler to ensure you have straight edges.

3

Score along the dotted lines, again using a ruler to make sure that your lines are straight.

4

Bend along the fold lines to pop out the star and create a 3D effect.

Gifts to give

Layered papercut

A framed papercut will look great on a wall or side table. Their best feature is their versatility—once you've mastered the basic technique, get creative and come up with your own designs.

Tracing paper

Selection of cardstock

Cutting mat

Ruler

Craft knife

Eraser

Foam pads

Pencil

Box photo frame

Masking tape

You will need

1 Cut the cardstock to size using the frame as a guide.

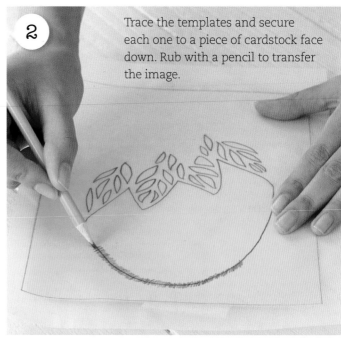

2 Trace the templates and secure each one to a piece of cardstock face down. Rub with a pencil to transfer the image.

3 Using a fresh blade, carefully cut out the small details.

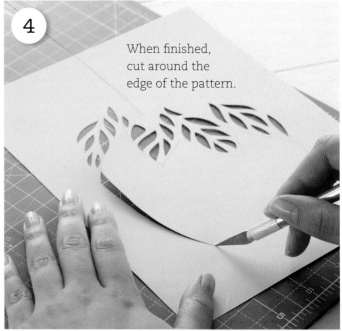

4 When finished, cut around the edge of the pattern.

5 Repeat with the other templates, then trace and cut out the oval.

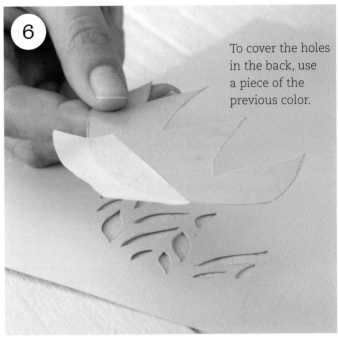

6 To cover the holes in the back, use a piece of the previous color.

7 Place foam pads around the edges and corners on the back of each layer to add depth.

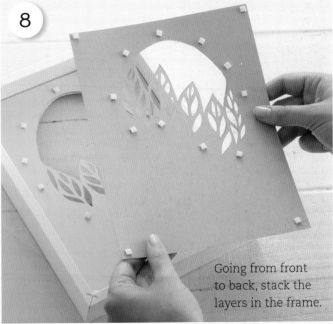

8 Going from front to back, stack the layers in the frame.

To vary the papercut, design your own template
using different flower shapes. Alternatively, you
can remove the foam pads to create a flat design.

Layered papercuts
can be made to suit
almost any frame.

Quilled earrings

The art of quilling has been around for centuries, but this modern twist makes for a perfect gift. You can easily customize the shapes to make your own designs.

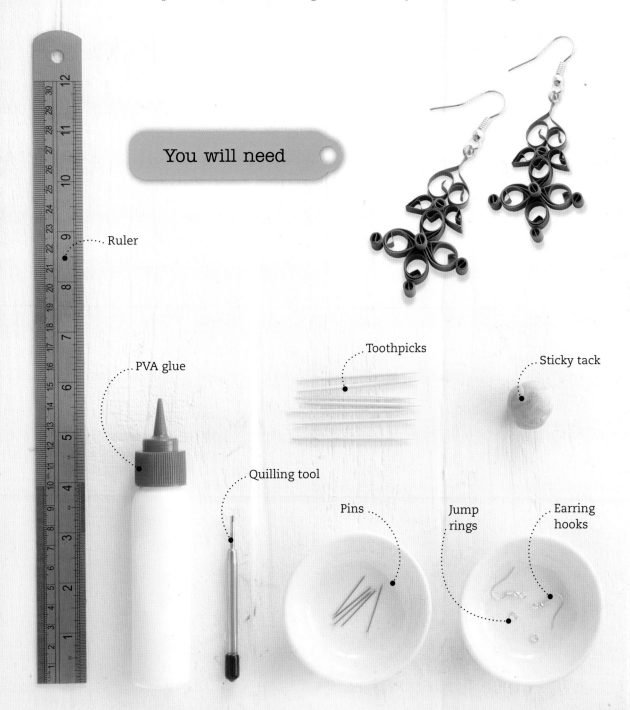

Dark and light strips of quilling paper

You will need

Ruler

PVA glue

Toothpicks

Sticky tack

Quilling tool

Pins

Jump rings

Earring hooks

1

Cut the dark green quilling strips into two 4in (10cm) and four 2in (5cm) strips. Then cut the light green strips into three 4in (10cm) and three 2in (5cm) strips.

2

Only glue near the bottom of the fold.

Take a long light green strip and fold it in half. Open it up and apply a little glue near the fold. This will form a base for you to attach the earrings to later on.

3

Insert one end of the strip into the tool and twist it toward the fold, leaving a small gap at the end. Release and repeat with the other side to create a heart.

When finished, glue together

4

Take a short light strip and twist it into a tight coil. Glue the end down and slide it off the tool. Repeat with the remaining short light strips and two dark ones.

5

Twirl one of the long dark strips into a coil, then release and glue in place.

Pinch one of the ends to make a teardrop shape. Repeat this with the remaining long and short strips.

6

Arrange your pieces on a surface, reserving one small coil. If you want to, you can try a different shape, but make sure it's strong enough to hold together.

7

Carefully glue the pieces together using a toothpick (tweezers can also help). Go slowly, allowing each piece to dry before adding the next.

Glue the reserved coil on top

8

Place the base of the heart on the sticky tack and use a pin to make a hole. Thread a jump ring through the hole and then attach an earring hook. Repeat for the second earring.

60

Nursery papercut

This charming papercut is deceptively simple to put together and would make a lovely decoration for a nursery or young child's bedroom. It's easily adaptable, so tailor your papercut's subject and size to whatever you wish.

You will need

Cutting mat

Ruler

Eraser

Frame

Pencil

Craft knife

White cardstock

Acetate

Tracing paper

Colored cardstock

Using a pencil, transfer the template to tracing paper and turn it over. Lay it on top of your cardstock and rub over the tracing with pencil to transfer the image onto the cardstock.

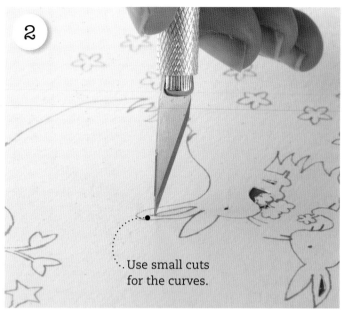

Use small cuts for the curves.

Using a fresh blade, carefully start cutting the smaller, more delicate areas of the picture such as the eyes, arms, and the inside of the ears.

Take your time to ensure the cuts are neat.

Working in a clockwise direction, cut one side of each petal at the bottom toward the center of each flower, then cut the other side of each petal working in the other direction.

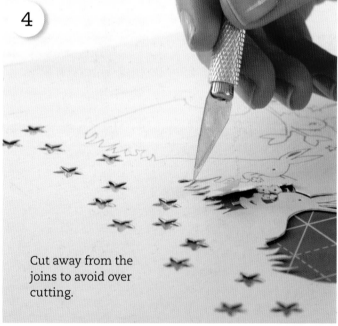

Cut away from the joins to avoid over cutting.

Turn the image upside down and cut out the grass. When this is complete, carefully cut away the remaining paper between the rabbits.

Working around the edges, begin to cut away the rest of the image. Take your time, especially with smaller areas such as the stars and leaves.

Once you have finished cutting away all of the images, flip the cardstock over and go back over any snagged areas to tidy them up

Measure the size of the glass in your frame and cut the image, acetate, and background cardstock to this size. Use the glass to ensure the image is central to the markings.

Place the glass and image in the frame, followed by the acetate. Add the frame insert and lay the background cardstock on top before affixing the back of the frame in place.

Papercut locket

With a little creativity, patience, and a very steady hand, you can adapt the same technique used for the nursery papercut to make something small enough to fit in a locket.

Almost any simple shape will work, but since the papercut needs to be small, choose something without too much detail or it will be very hard to cut neatly.

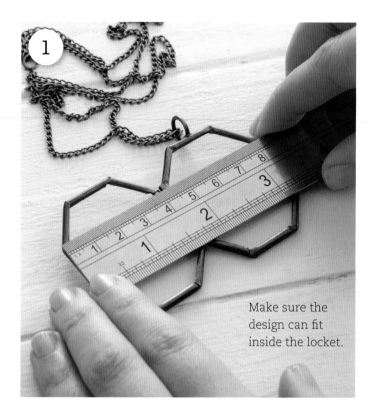

Make sure the design can fit inside the locket.

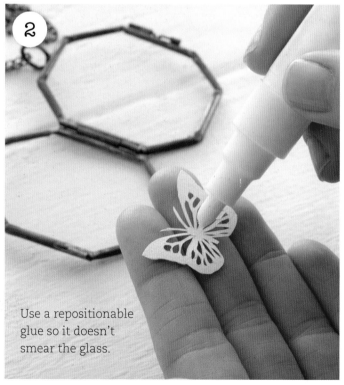

Use a repositionable glue so it doesn't smear the glass.

Papercut lantern

These stylish hand-cut lanterns will produce a lovely, gentle glow and will look great on any mantelpiece. They also make perfect table decorations for a dinner party or wedding.

Ruler

Tracing paper

Cutting mat

Double-sided tape

Strong paper

You will need

Pencil

Craft knife

1

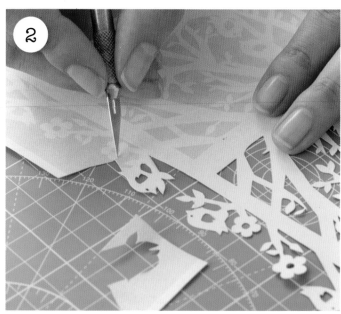

2

Prepare your template and begin to cut away the inside of one of the four panels. Make sure you keep the template right-side up during the whole cutting process.

Once you've finished cutting the inside of the first panel, cut out the pattern above it. Repeat this process, going from one side of the template to the other.

3

4

Continue until all of the excess paper has been cut away. You may need to change your blade several times to avoid creating frayed edges.

Apply thin double-sided tape to the edges of the panels. Before peeling off the second side, measure and cut four tracing paper rectangles the same size as the tape's border.

Peel back the other half of the tape and carefully stick the tracing paper on top. Repeat this process until the tracing paper covers all four panels.

Fold all of the flaps and side lines, making sure that there's a stiff crease on all the edges. This will ensure that the lantern will stand up straight when finished.

Glue or tape all of the flaps in place, holding them in position for a short while to make sure they stick properly. To finish, add a flameless candle or fairy lights.

You can also create papercut lanterns by
wrapping colored tracing paper around
a vase and placing the papercut on top.

Don't feel like you have to only make dark silhouettes. These also work surprisingly well with brightly-colored cardstock.

Silhouette frame

A modern take on the classic family portrait, a silhouette gallery is simple to put together and can make an instant impression. They're also a great way to repurpose old photos.

You will need

- Dark cardstock
- Cutting mat
- Tracing paper
- Light cardstock
- Scissors
- Glue stick
- Ruler
- Craft knife
- Pen
- Frames
- Photos

1 Trace around the outline of your photo.

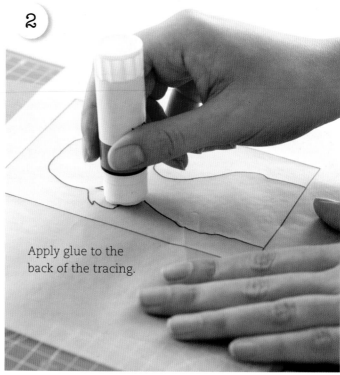

2 Apply glue to the back of the tracing.

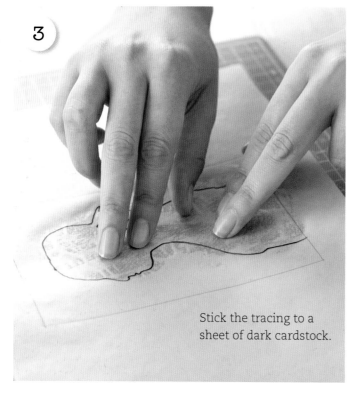

3 Stick the tracing to a sheet of dark cardstock.

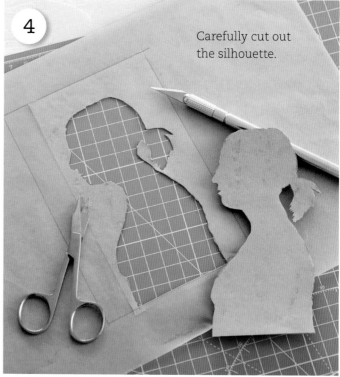

4 Carefully cut out the silhouette.

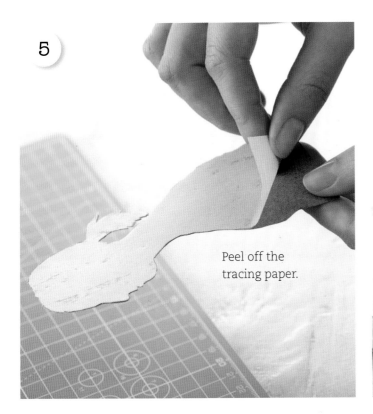

5

Peel off the
tracing paper.

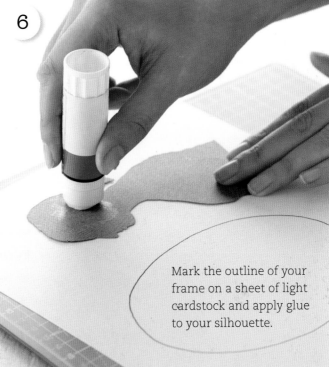

6

Mark the outline of your
frame on a sheet of light
cardstock and apply glue
to your silhouette.

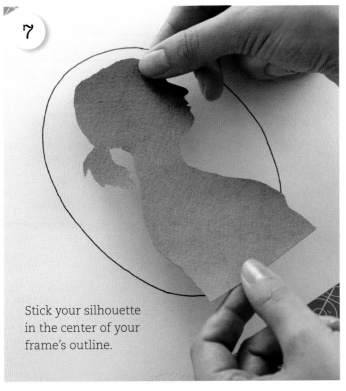

7

Stick your silhouette
in the center of your
frame's outline.

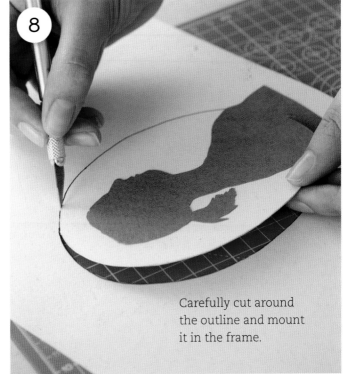

8

Carefully cut around
the outline and mount
it in the frame.

Decorations

Honeycomb pom-pom

These appealing pom-poms can liven up any room, and are perfect for a party, wedding, or just as decorations for a room. They work well in both bright and pastel colors.

You will need

Two colors of tissue paper

Cutting mat

Ruler

Scissors

Bodkin

Double-sided tape

Paper clips

Pencil and colored pens

Paper

Cardstock

Strong needle and thread

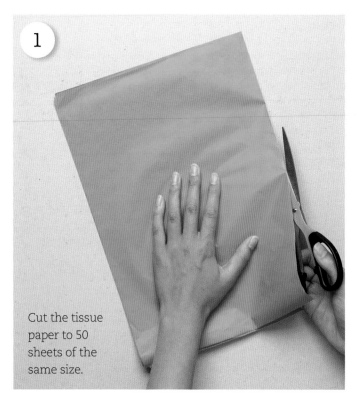

1

Cut the tissue paper to 50 sheets of the same size.

2

Cut a sheet of cardstock slightly larger than your sheets. Mark the top and bottom edges, leaving a ½in (1cm) border, then divide the space inside into five equally-spaced lines.

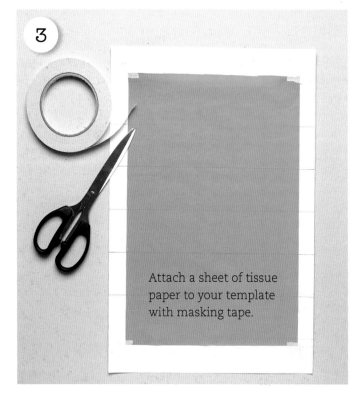

3

Attach a sheet of tissue paper to your template with masking tape.

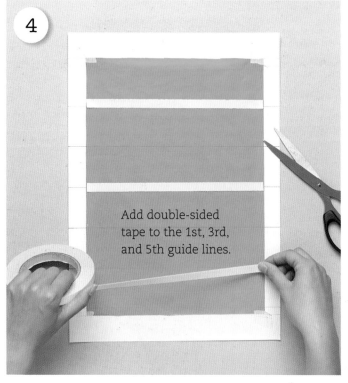

4

Add double-sided tape to the 1st, 3rd, and 5th guide lines.

5 Stick down five sheets of one color, then three of another, alternating between the odd and even guide lines every time.

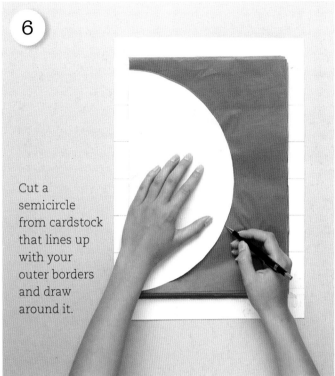

6 Cut a semicircle from cardstock that lines up with your outer borders and draw around it.

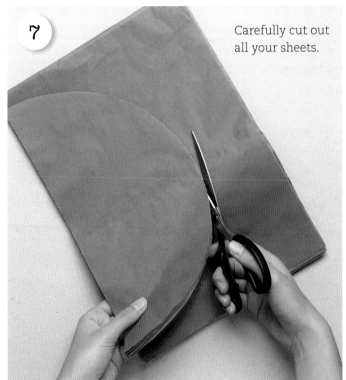

7 Carefully cut out all your sheets.

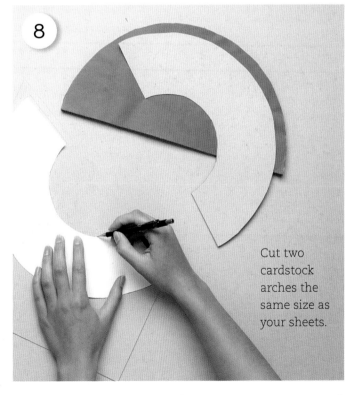

8 Cut two cardstock arches the same size as your sheets.

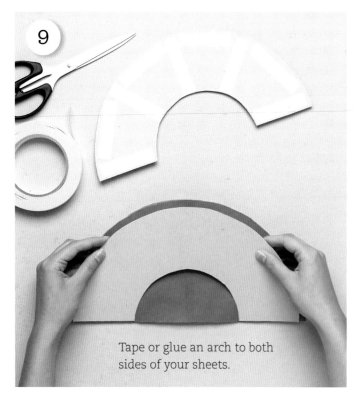

9

Tape or glue an arch to both sides of your sheets.

10

Poke a hole at both ends with a bodkin or thick pin.

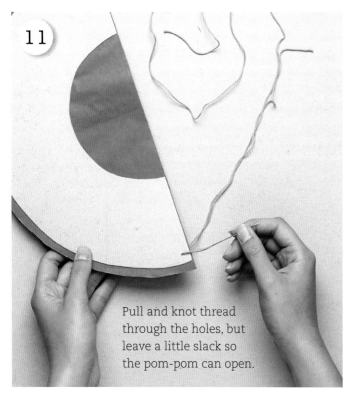

11

Pull and knot thread through the holes, but leave a little slack so the pom-pom can open.

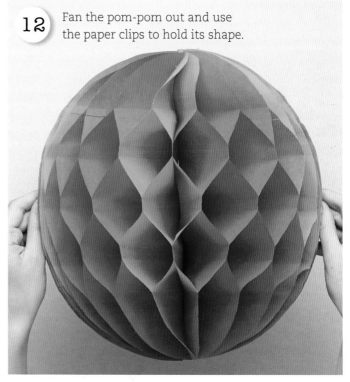

12

Fan the pom-pom out and use the paper clips to hold its shape.

13

Hang the pom-
poms from the
knotted thread.

Origami fairy lights

Whether the holiday season is right around the corner or you're just looking to brighten up a room, these fairy lights will do the trick. Depending how strong your LED lights are, you may need to experiment with a variety of paper opacity to get the right look.

You will need

Squares of thin paper

LED fairy lights

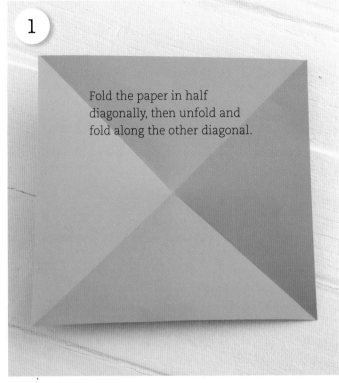

1 Fold the paper in half diagonally, then unfold and fold along the other diagonal.

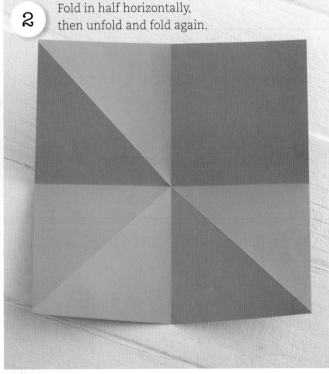

2 Fold in half horizontally, then unfold and fold again.

3 Turn the paper over.

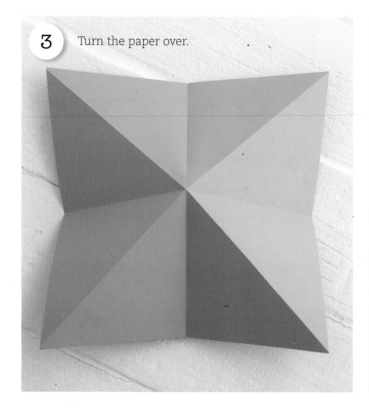

4 Push in the right and left horizontal folds, then flatten to create a layered triangle shape.

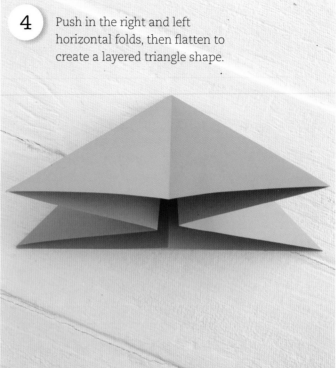

5 Fold up the bottom corners as shown, then repeat on the back to form a diamond.

6

Fold the front edges inward as shown, then repeat on the back.

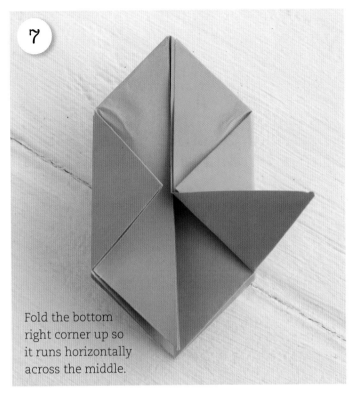

7

Fold the bottom right corner up so it runs horizontally across the middle.

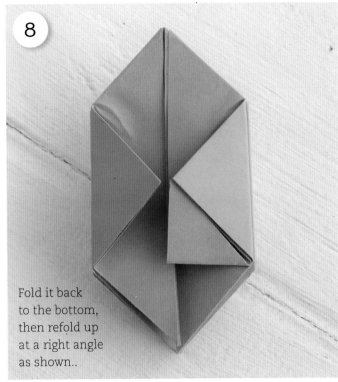

8

Fold it back to the bottom, then refold up at a right angle as shown..

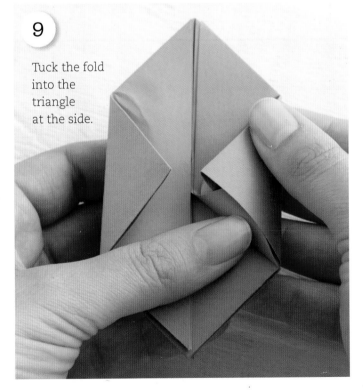

9

Tuck the fold into the triangle at the side.

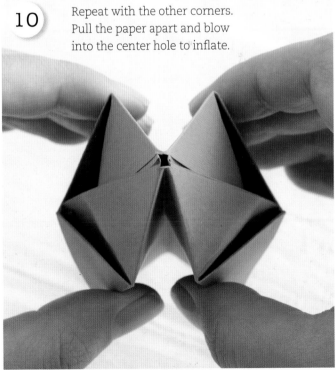

10

Repeat with the other corners. Pull the paper apart and blow into the center hole to inflate.

Hanging fan

These bright, bold fans can take a while to put together, but the results are stunning. By making several in a variety of colors and sizes, you'll be able to create a striking wall display.

You will need

Assorted buttons and beads

Hot glue gun and sticks

Selection of paper

Ruler

Utility knife

Scorer

Pen

PVA glue and brush

Greaseproof paper

Glue stick

Sticky tape

Assorted ribbons

Cutting mat

Score equally-spaced vertical lines on several sheets of paper. The more sheets you use and the wider the lines, the bigger the fan will be. Use the guides on your cutting mat to make sure the lines are straight.

Apply PVA glue to the bottom segment of one of the sheets of paper. Stick the top segment of another sheet of paper on top so they overlap. Allow to dry and then repeat with the other sheets (minimum of two).

Fold the paper along the scored creases to create an accordion effect.

Repeat this process with slimmer sheets of paper that are a different color. When done, lay them flat and cut shapes into the folds to add detail.

5

Repeat again with another thinner paper. However, instead of cutting a design in the folds, slice the ends off diagonally.

6

Use a glue stick to attach the second paper to the first and allow to dry. Now apply glue to the bottom of the third.

7

Glue the third paper along the bottom edge of the fan. Take your time to ensure the edges align properly.

Make sure to glue firmly.

Apply PVA glue to one of the ends, then bring the two sides of the accordion together to form a large circle.

Lay the fan on the greaseproof paper and use a hot glue gun to create a pool of glue in the center.

Using both hands, carefully squeeze the fan inward so the center moves toward the glue and shrinks. Hold in place until the glue sets, then peel away the greaseproof paper.

Use the inside ring of a roll of sticky tape to mark two discs from cardstock. One should be plain, and the other one should have colored paper stuck to it. Neatly cut out the discs.

12 Turn the fan on its back and stick the plain disc to the center with hot glue. Fold a ribbon in half, place the opposite ends on top, then stick the second disc on top with more hot glue.

13 Lay the folded ribbon between one of the fan's folds, then secure in place with a strip of paper and some PVA glue.

14 Cover the hole on the front of your fan with buttons or beads.

Hanging garlands

Garlands are a simple but effective decoration for any party or celebration. You can use colored papers that match your theme, but they can also be made from pretty scraps.

Paper

PVA glue and brush

String

Scissors

Beads

3in (7.5cm) circle punch

Glue stick

You will need

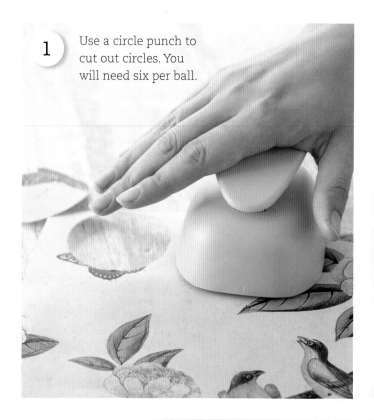

1 Use a circle punch to cut out circles. You will need six per ball.

2 Fold the circles in half, image sides together.

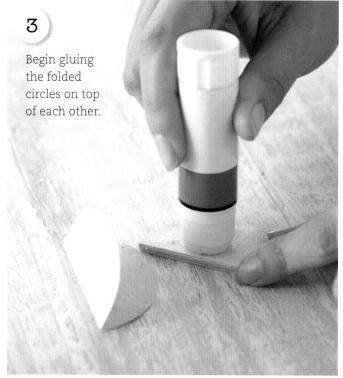

3 Begin gluing the folded circles on top of each other.

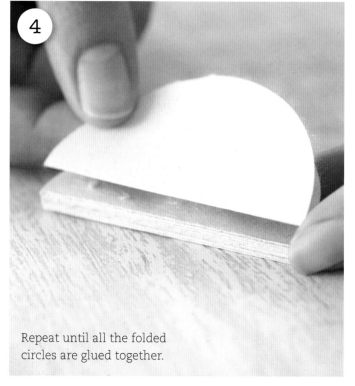

4 Repeat until all the folded circles are glued together.

5 Make two knots on a length of string and glue it between the circles. Close the circles around the string and glue in place.

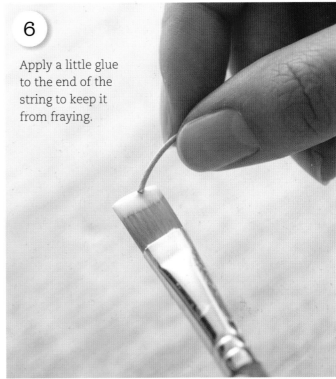

6 Apply a little glue to the end of the string to keep it from fraying.

7 Thread beads onto the string and make a loop at the end.

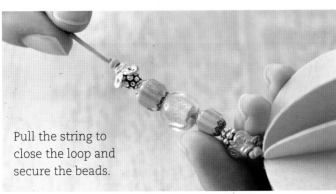

Pull the string to close the loop and secure the beads.

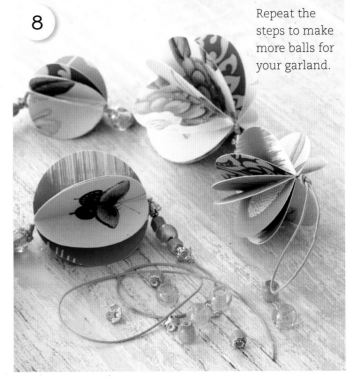

8 Repeat the steps to make more balls for your garland.

Snowflake ornament

A simple but pretty winter decoration, these snowflakes can be hung from string or ribbon to great effect. However, they look even better when encased in ornaments and placed on a tree.

Clear plastic ornaments

Cutting mat

Brush

Craft knife

Pencil

PVA glue

White paper or cardstock

Tracing paper

Scrap surface

You will need

1 Trace four templates and place them face down on the paper or cardstock. Rub to transfer.

2

Carefully cut out the snowflakes.

3 Fold the snowflakes in half as shown, being careful to align the edges.

4

Apply glue to one side of the folded shape.

Glue one of the shapes to another, then repeat to create a 3D shape.

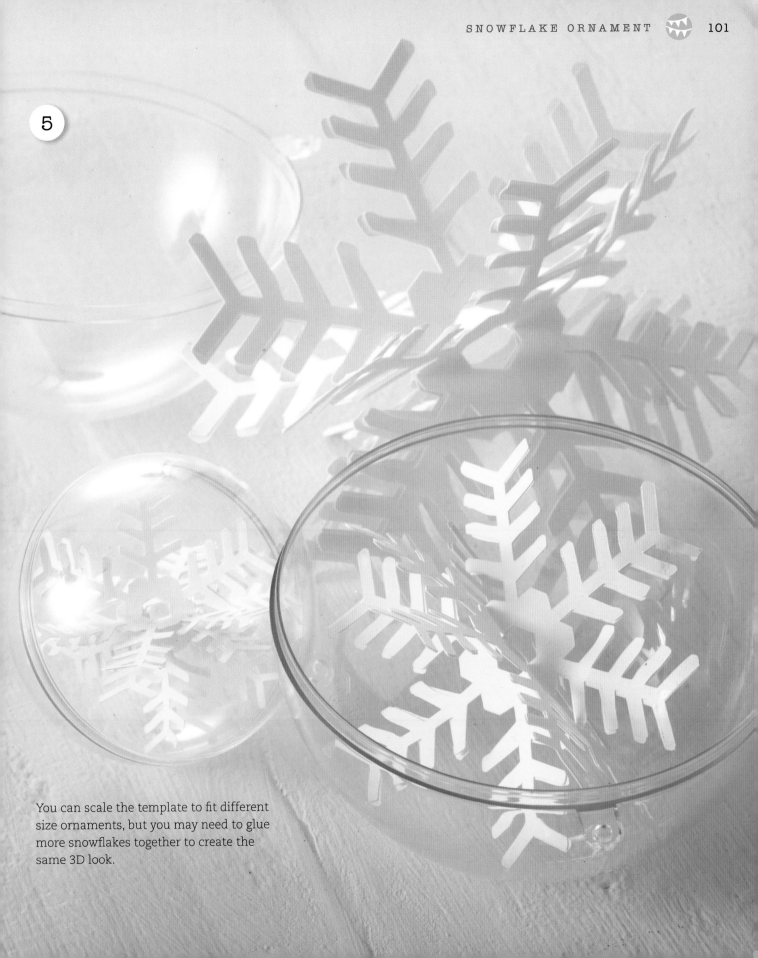

5

You can scale the template to fit different size ornaments, but you may need to glue more snowflakes together to create the same 3D look.

Kids' crafts

Origami bird

These cute little birds are easy to put together and make great decorations. You can also put paper leaves in their beaks and use them as placeholders at a dinner party.

Craft knife

2½in (6cm) circle punch

Cutting mat

Scissors

Hole punch

Squares of paper

Hot glue gun and sticks

Glue

Spray mount

Ruler

You will need

1 Fold the paper in half diagonally.

Open, then fold two sides in as shown.

2 Turn the paper over and fold the top down.

Turn it back over and fold down the corners.

3 Lift up each flap, pull the top corner to the side, then fold back down as shown.

Tuck the corners underneath so they poke out a little.

4 Fold the bird in half so that the open fold is at the top, then fold the middle in to create a beak.

5

Fold the tail along the top toward the head.

Unfold and refold at the base of the head to create a crease.

6

Open up the tail and fold the bottom section inside using the crease lines as a guide.

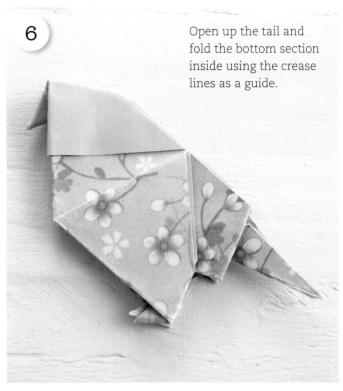

7

Cut out a disc of cardstock with a circle punch. Stick the bird's feet to the disc using hot glue.

8

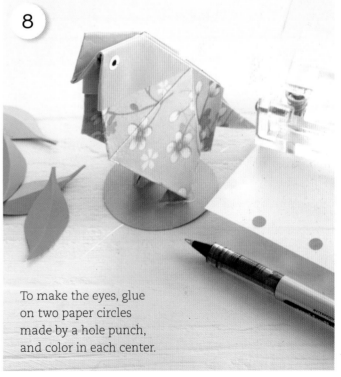

To make the eyes, glue on two paper circles made by a hole punch, and color in each center.

Animal mask

Simple to make and fun for kids, you can adapt
the basic technique for this bear mask to create
a dog, a monkey, or almost any creature from
the animal kingdom.

Marker pens

Colored
cardstock

Pencil

Tracing paper

Scrap surface

Brush

Scissors

Glue

Scorer

You will need

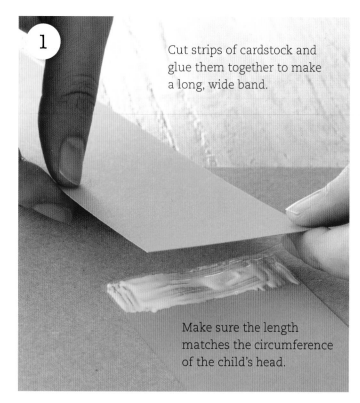

1 Cut strips of cardstock and glue them together to make a long, wide band.

Make sure the length matches the circumference of the child's head.

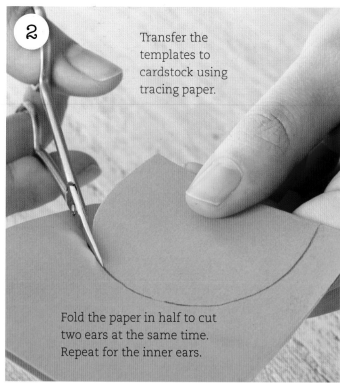

2 Transfer the templates to cardstock using tracing paper.

Fold the paper in half to cut two ears at the same time. Repeat for the inner ears.

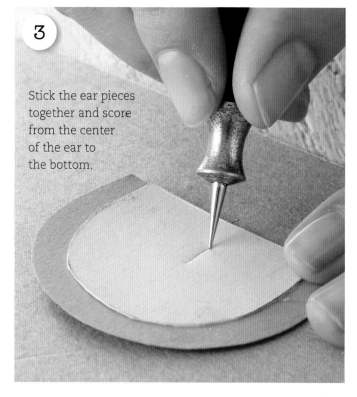

3 Stick the ear pieces together and score from the center of the ear to the bottom.

4 Using the score mark, fold the ear to give it a slightly curved shape. Glue in place.

5

Using the template, cut the patches that go around the eyes.

Measure the distance between the eyes and mark them on the band.

6

Cut out the nose and mouth pieces. Glue together, then stick to the front of the band.

Color inside the eyes to avoid an orange line when they are cut out.

7

Cut out the eye holes and glue the ears to the back of the mask.

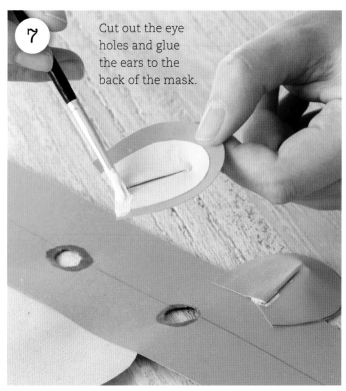

8

Carefully draw around the outside edge of the mouthpiece.

Owl mobile

This cheerful mobile is the perfect decoration to hang above a child's bed. The basic design is fairly easy to adapt, so it's a great project to personalize and give as a gift.

You will need

Paper and cardstock

Double-sided tape

Cutting mat

Embroidery hoop

Masking tape

Scorer

Pencil

Craft knife

Sticky pads

White thread

Beads

Scissors

Glittered cardstock

Dark thread

Metallic cardstock

Tracing paper

Making the owls

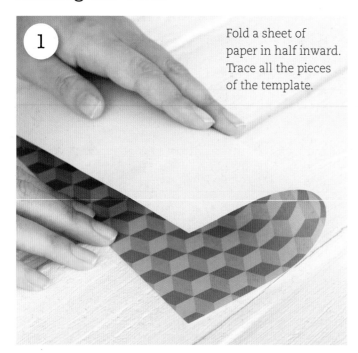

1 Fold a sheet of paper in half inward. Trace all the pieces of the template.

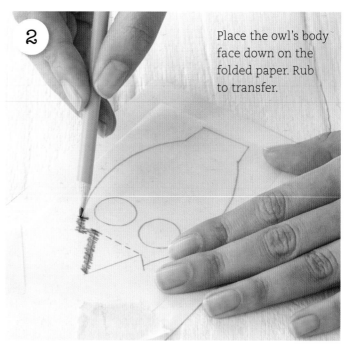

2 Place the owl's body face down on the folded paper. Rub to transfer.

3 Cut out the eyes and bodies to make two halves of your owl.

4 Transfer and cut out all the other template pieces.

5 Cut "U" shapes into the breast to make feathers.

Gently fold and push out the feathers.

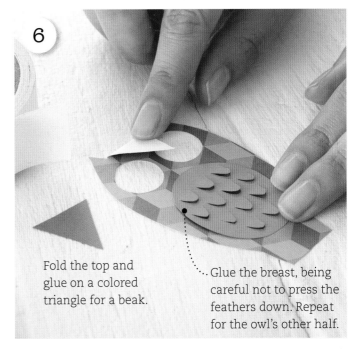

6 Fold the top and glue on a colored triangle for a beak.

Glue the breast, being careful not to press the feathers down. Repeat for the owl's other half.

7 Stick thin strips of double-sided tape above and below the eyes, then stretch a piece of cotton thread between them.

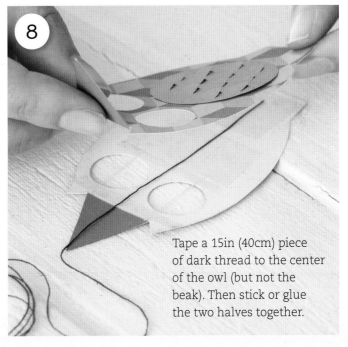

8 Tape a 15in (40cm) piece of dark thread to the center of the owl (but not the beak). Then stick or glue the two halves together.

9 Use double-sided tape or glue to attach the wings to the body.

10 Cut four circles and glue to either side of the thread between the eyes. Secure the beak with a sticky pad.

11 Roll a piece of paper around a pencil and glue to make a branch. Remove the pencil.

12 Attach leaves with tape or glue.

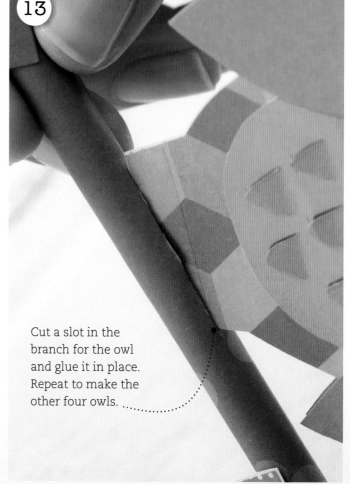

13 Cut a slot in the branch for the owl and glue it in place. Repeat to make the other four owls.

Assembling the mobile

1

Cut stars from glittery paper and tape over the thread hanging above the owls.

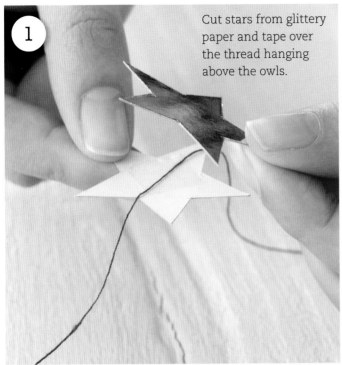

2

Fold metallic paper in half and cut 12 semicircles at the folded edge.

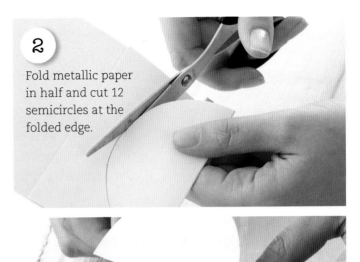

Stick the folded circles on top of each other.

3

Tie a bead to a piece of thread and place it in the seam between the circles.

Stick the final pieces of the circle together to form a ball.

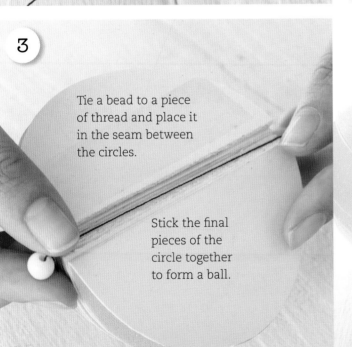

4

Paint the embroidery hoop and tie thread across its diameter four times.

Tie the ball where the threads meet, leaving a slight drop, then tie the owls to the hoop.

Party crown

Fun and diverse, paper crowns can be made to suit any dress-up costume or party theme. Try adapting the basic template to create your own designs.

Cutting mat

Craft knife

Ruler

Brush

PVA glue

Double-sided sticky pads

Tracing paper

String

Cardstock

Pencil

Scissors

You will need

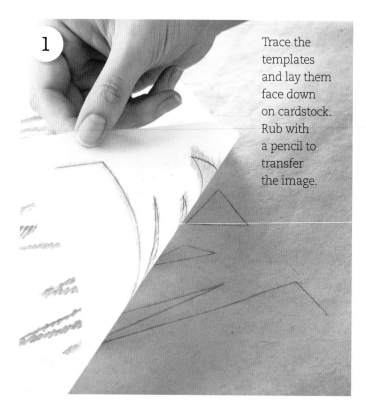

1 Trace the templates and lay them face down on cardstock. Rub with a pencil to transfer the image.

2 Cut out the shapes with a craft knife, using a ruler to make sure the cuts are straight.

3 Apply glue to the points of the crown.

4 Stick the other cardstock on top so the two pieces properly align.

5

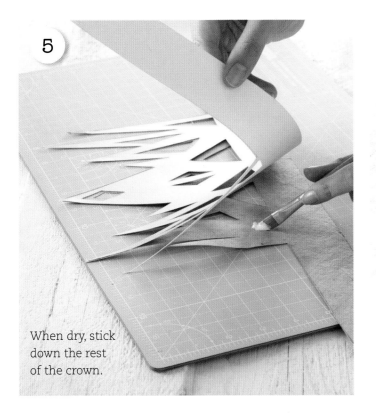

When dry, stick
down the rest
of the crown.

6

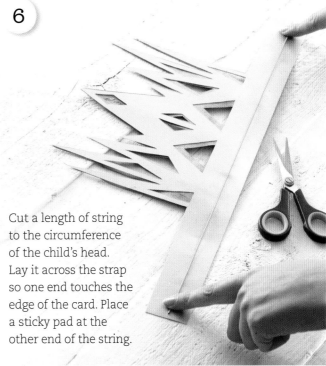

Cut a length of string
to the circumference
of the child's head.
Lay it across the strap
so one end touches the
edge of the card. Place
a sticky pad at the
other end of the string.

7

Peel the back
off the sticky
pad and stick
down the strap.

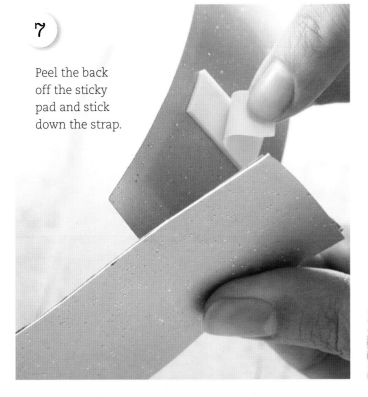

8 Trim and neaten any
overhang or rough edges.

Flowers

Cherry blossom

While most popular in Japan, cherry blossoms are a symbol of renewal and growth all over the world. This gorgeous paper version will make you feel like spring is always just around the corner.

Crepe paper

Cardstock

Cutting mat

Scrap surface

Hot glue gun and glue stick

Scissors

Dry branches

Pencil

Glue

You will need

1

Trace the templates and place
upside down on cardstock.
Rub with a pencil to transfer.

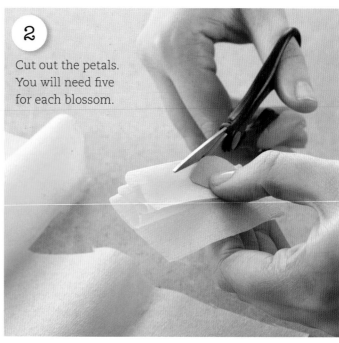

2

Cut out the petals.
You will need five
for each blossom.

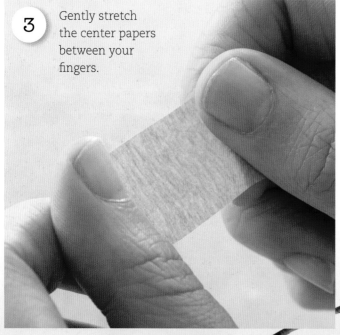

3

Gently stretch
the center papers
between your
fingers.

4

Fringe the center papers
finely, about ½in (1cm) deep.

Roll the centers
between your fingers
and glue the opposite ends.

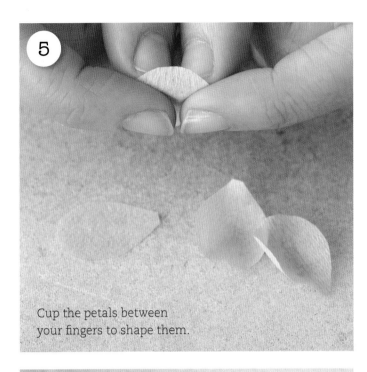

Cup the petals between
your fingers to shape them.

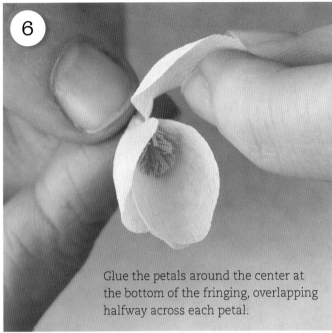

Glue the petals around the center at
the bottom of the fringing, overlapping
halfway across each petal.

Once dry, cut
the stems to
¼in (0.5cm).

Gently squeeze the petals
down to form the blossom.

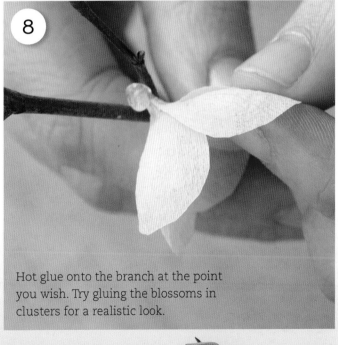

Hot glue onto the branch at the point
you wish. Try gluing the blossoms in
clusters for a realistic look.

Peony

Prized for their size and petal count, peonies are one of the most popular flowers in the world. And while paper versions can't replicate their scent, they definitely deliver the wow factor.

20-gauge florist wire

Ruler

Crepe paper

Glue

Pencil

Spray mount

Scissors

Pliers

Tracing paper

You will need

1

Cut three different-colored
2½x 1½in (6 x 4cm) sheets of crepe
paper and stack on top of each other.

2

Cut fringe halfway
through the paper and
crumple the ends.

Place florist wire at one
end and add glue. Roll
the paper around the wire.

3

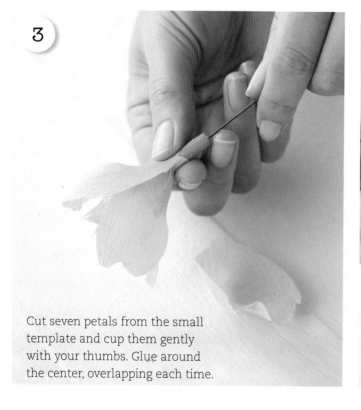

Cut seven petals from the small
template and cup them gently
with your thumbs. Glue around
the center, overlapping each time.

4

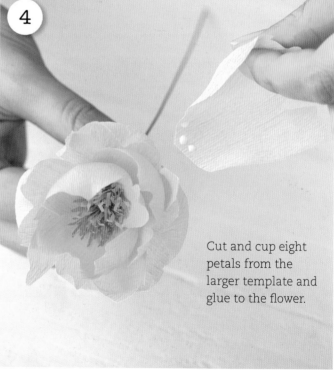

Cut and cup eight
petals from the
larger template and
glue to the flower.

5

Cut and glue three green pieces of paper at the bottom for the calyx.

6

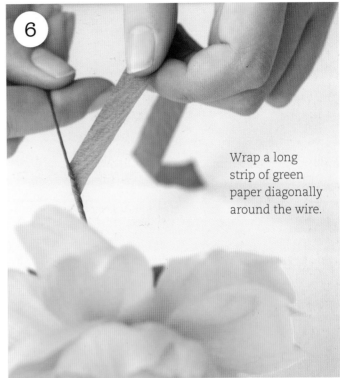

Wrap a long strip of green paper diagonally around the wire.

7

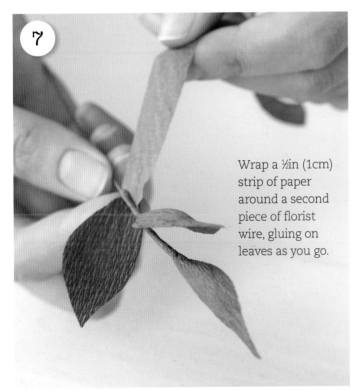

Wrap a ½in (1cm) strip of paper around a second piece of florist wire, gluing on leaves as you go.

8

Glue the two pieces of wire together and wrap with more paper to secure.

Ranunculus

Known for their delicate petals and brilliant colors, a ranunculus arrangement can breathe life into any room. This simple and beautiful paper version is no exception.

Pencil

Cutting mat

20-gauge florist wire

Wire cutters

Scissors

Cardstock

Hot glue gun and glue stick

½in (1.5cm) polystyrene balls

You will need

Glue

Crepe paper

Place a little hot glue on the end of a piece of floral wire and insert it into the center of a polystyrene ball. Glue a small dark green circle on top of the ball, then cut out 15 light green petals using template 1.

Cut floral wire to the desired length.

Cup each petal between your thumb and forefinger and apply glue to the bottom. Glue a petal so the curved edge almost meets the center of the ball, then overlap five more by 50 percent so they curve away from the one before.

Add the remaining green petals, but layer them slightly higher than before. Cut out and cup 11 yellow petals from the same template and overlap these on top of the green petals, bringing them slightly higher.

Cut out the orange petals. You will need 21 from template 2 and 18 from template 3. These petals need to have a deeper cup than the yellow or green ones.

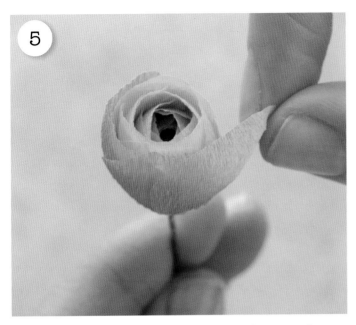

Add a little glue to the bottom of the petals from template 2 and begin gluing them to the flower slightly higher than the yellow layer. Continue overlapping as you go, bringing the layers down slightly as the flower begins to take shape.

Glue the petals from template 3 so that the base of each petal touches the stem and covers any remaining areas of the polystyrene ball. Continue overlapping these petals around the flower.

To make the calyx, cut four pieces of green crepe paper and slightly cup in the middle to give them a little shape. Glue the end of the calyx shapes to the foot of the stem.

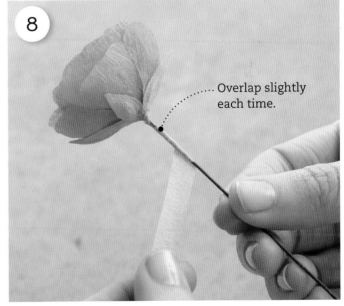

Overlap slightly each time.

Cut a strip of paper across the grain about ½in (1cm) wide and stretch it out. Glue one end under the calyx and wind the paper around the wire, applying a little glue every six or so turns. Repeat until the stem is your desired thickness.

Daisy

These bright and cheerful daisies add a touch of spring to any room. Although they are made of paper, their white petals and yellow centers manage to look quite realistic.

Glue

Spray mount

Scrap surface

Pliers

Pencil

Tracing paper

Wire

20 and 26-gauge florist wire

Crepe paper

Ruler

Scissors

Watercolor paints

You will need

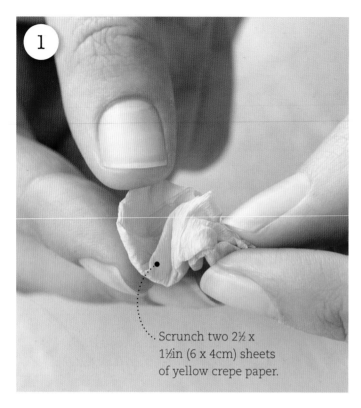

1

Scrunch two 2½ x 1½in (6 x 4cm) sheets of yellow crepe paper.

2

Push florist wire into the paper and glue another square of crepe paper around it.

Squeeze until it holds its shape.

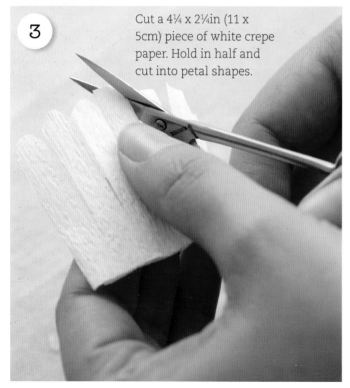

3

Cut a 4¼ x 2¼in (11 x 5cm) piece of white crepe paper. Hold in half and cut into petal shapes.

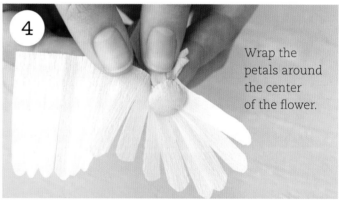

4

Wrap the petals around the center of the flower.

Bind to the stem with 26-gauge wire. Use pliers if you have trouble keeping it tight.

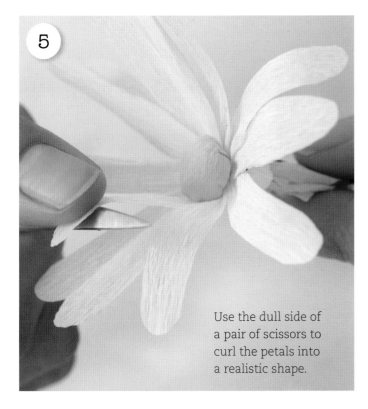

5

Use the dull side of a pair of scissors to curl the petals into a realistic shape.

6

Trim away the excess yellow paper at the top of the stem.

7

Wind a ½in (1cm) strip of crepe paper around the wire a few times. Cut leaves and glue to the wire, then wrap another green strip around to secure.

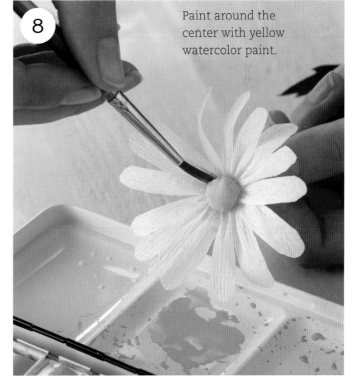

8

Paint around the center with yellow watercolor paint.

Anemone

You can make amazing paper anemones in a variety of shades, from pale pink and lilac to a rich jewel-like purple. Their delicate crepe paper petals are almost impossible to distinguish from the real thing.

Brush

Pencil

Watercolor

Wire

Scissors

Pliers

Scrap surface

Tracing paper

Crepe paper

20-gauge florist wire

Spray mount

Glue

You will need

Ruler

Cut two squares of black crepe paper, then cut one in half. Stretch out the square, then scrunch one of the rectangles into a ball and wrap the other rectangle around it.

Hold in place until dry.

Place the ball of crepe paper in the middle of the stretched square and dot small amounts of glue around it. Holding the center down with straight floral wire, pull the corners of the square up around the scrunched paper and wire.

Cut a strip of purple crepe paper about 2in (5cm) long and fringe two-thirds of it. Wrap it around the black center and glue in place, then secure with wire and paint the tips black.

Using the template, cut six petal shapes from the purple crepe paper. Push your thumbs into the center and gently stretch outward to give them a rounded shape.

Dab glue around the base of the cut petals and attach them to the stalk, overlapping slightly. Once the glue has dried, cut away the excess black crepe paper below the petals.

Wrap the base of the flower with a long strip of green crepe paper and then wrap it down the stem diagonally. Glue in place at the bottom. Repeat until the stem is thick enough.

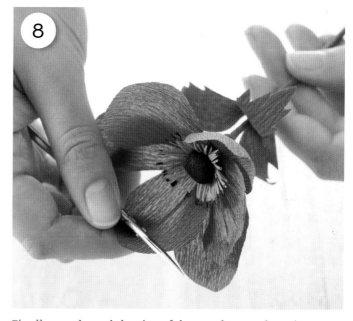

Use the template to cut four leaves from green crepe paper. Curl the leaves with scissors to give them a realistic shape, then glue them to the stem underneath the flower.

Finally, gently curl the tips of the petals over the scissors so that they curve inward.

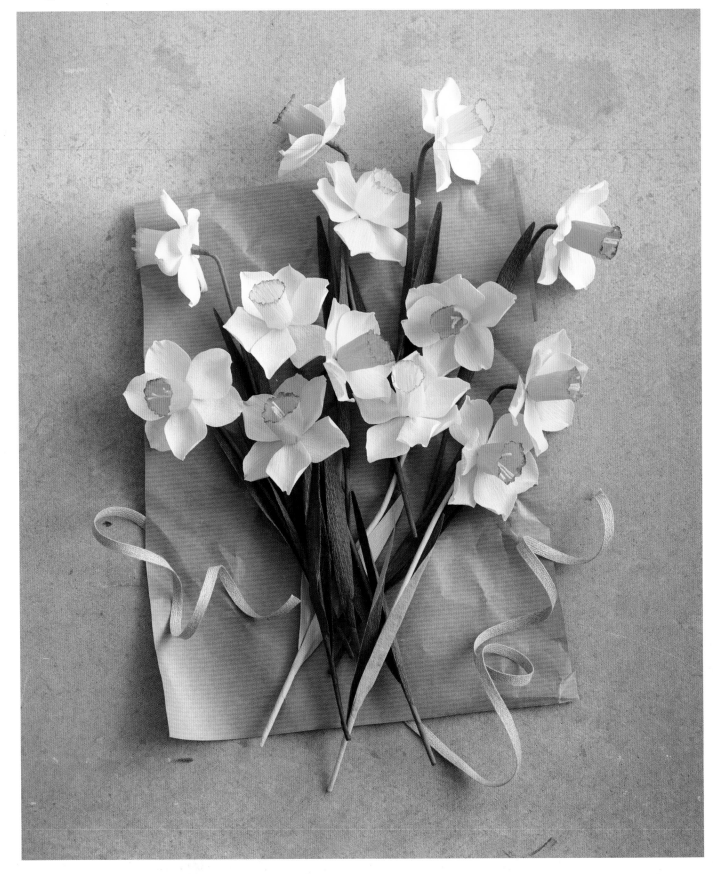

Daffodil

These bright and cheerful daffodils are simple to make and will last a lot longer than the real thing. With their natural looking yellow petals, you can imagine it's spring all year long!

Glue

Spray mount

Pencil

Crepe paper

You will need

Wire

Watercolor paints

Ruler

Wire

Scissors

Scrap surface

Paintbrush

Pliers

Tracing paper

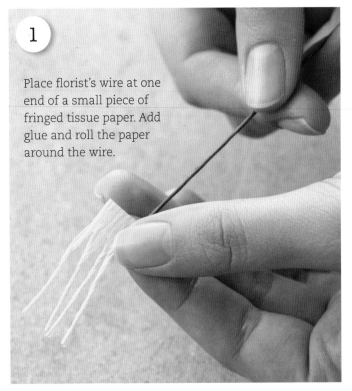

1 Place florist's wire at one end of a small piece of fringed tissue paper. Add glue and roll the paper around the wire.

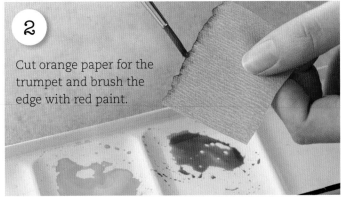

2 Cut orange paper for the trumpet and brush the edge with red paint.

Once dry, wrap the trumpet around the stamens and secure with wire.

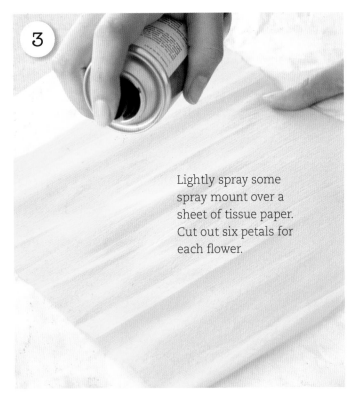

3 Lightly spray some spray mount over a sheet of tissue paper. Cut out six petals for each flower.

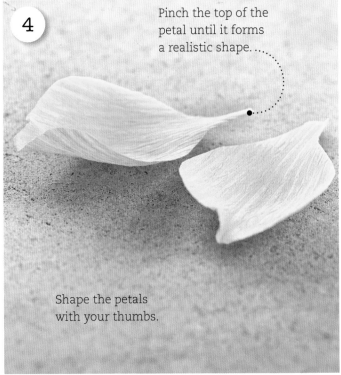

4 Pinch the top of the petal until it forms a realistic shape.

Shape the petals with your thumbs.

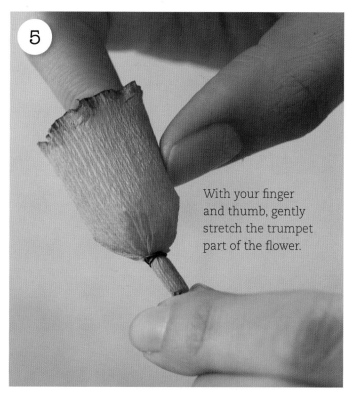

5 With your finger and thumb, gently stretch the trumpet part of the flower.

6 Arrange the petals around the stem. Diagonally wrap strips of green paper around to hold in place.

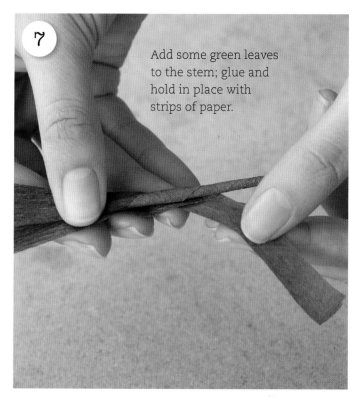

7 Add some green leaves to the stem; glue and hold in place with strips of paper.

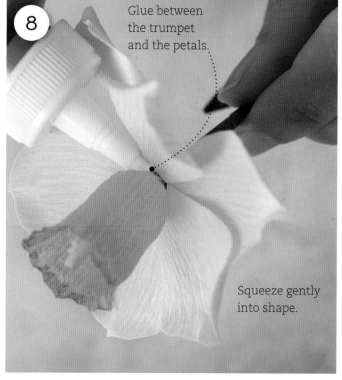

8 Glue between the trumpet and the petals.

Squeeze gently into shape.

Large rose

Perfect for a wedding or birthday party, these giant roses will make a beautiful statement. The dramatic and delicate petals make them look stunning and appealing.

You will need

Crepe paper and cardboard

Dowel rod

Round pencil

Stem tape

Scissors

Hot glue gun and sticks

Strong florist wire

Trace the templates on cardboard and cut them out. Draw around them and cut out six small, ten medium, and six large petals from pink crepe paper. Then cut eight sepals and one large leaf from dark green crepe paper.

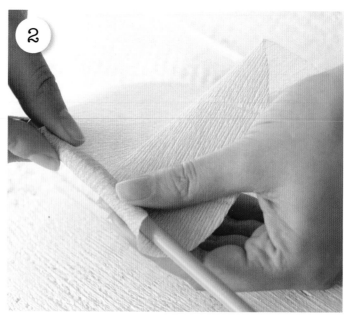

Put two small petals to one side, then use a pencil to curl the tips of the remaining petals. Stretch the paper slightly as you roll it. For the large petals, roll each lobe separately.

Push your thumbs into the center of the small petals to cup them. Push out the medium and large petals in the same way, but this time at three points on the petal.

Add a dab of hot glue to the bottom point of the two small, uncurled petals and attach them to the dowel rod. Apply glue to the top of the rod and roll the petals into a spiral around it.

Going from small to large, attach the remaining petals in the same way, spacing by eye. Add glue further up the petal to keep the shape if need be. You also may have to stretch the base of the large petals to fit.

For the sepals, slightly stretch the bottom of each one so that they fit around the base of the flower head. Then curl the points and glue them on, ensuring that some of the paper attaches to the dowel rod.

Place a line of hot glue along the center of the large green leaf and attach the floral wire. Fold the leaf in half and allow the hot glue to set before opening again.

Starting at the base of the rose, wind the stem tape around the dowel rod. After a few turns, add the wired leaf and glue it in place with the glue gun. Continue to wrap the stem tape around the rod until you reach the end.

Kusudama

These beautiful origami flowers are surprisingly simple to make and will liven up any room. They sit perfectly in a vase, but you can stick them to almost anything with a little glue.

You will need

Squares of paper

Glue

1

Choose your paper color. You'll need five squares per flower.

2

Fold into a triangle.

Fold both the bottom corners up to the middle.

3

Fold the points back so they line up with the outside edges.

4

Poke a finger inside each flap to pop them out, then flatten along the seam to create two kite shapes.

5

Fold the top triangle of the kite shapes flat so they are level with the long edge behind.

6

Fold the sides in to create a square shape.

7

Bring the two sides together to create a petal. Glue in place.

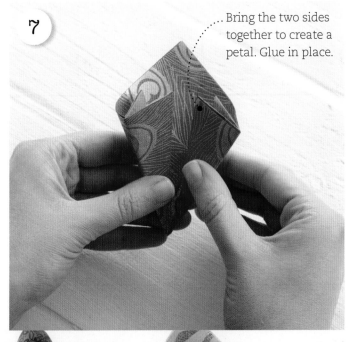

8

Repeat until you have five petals, then glue them together along the folds one at a time.

Wreath

Making a wreath is a great way to bring together all the flowers you have created into a single display. Try different combinations to get the effect that suits your home.

Ranunculuses

Anemones

Ruler

Crepe paper

18 and 26-gauge florist wire

Scrap surface

Pencil

Pliers

Spray mount

Tracing paper

Peonies

Daffodils

PVA Glue

Daisies

Scissors

You will need

1 Using stretched crepe paper ⅝in (1.5cm) wide, wrap three 14¼in (36cm) lengths of 18-gauge wire together to form a circle, overlapping by 3in (7.5cm) at each end.

2 Spray mount two shades of green crepe together and cut out around 60 leaves using the template.

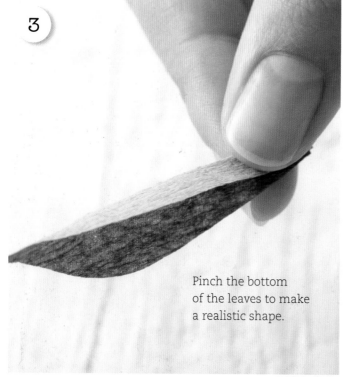

3 Pinch the bottom of the leaves to make a realistic shape.

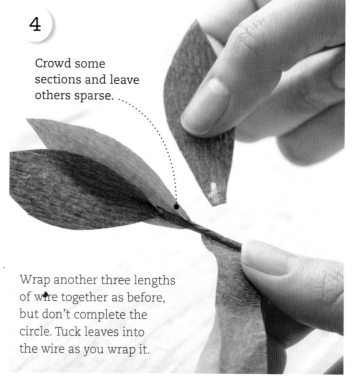

Crowd some sections and leave others sparse.

4 Wrap another three lengths of wire together as before, but don't complete the circle. Tuck leaves into the wire as you wrap it.

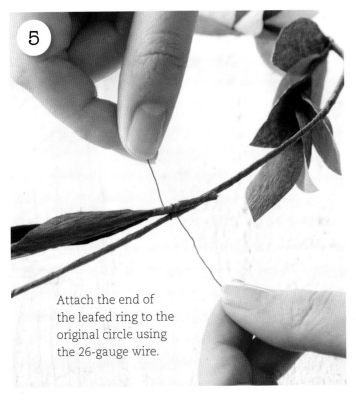

5 Attach the end of the leafed ring to the original circle using the 26-gauge wire.

6 Bend the leafed ring around the original circle, attaching it at various points using 26-gauge wire.

7 Use 26-gauge wire to attach flowers to the wreath.

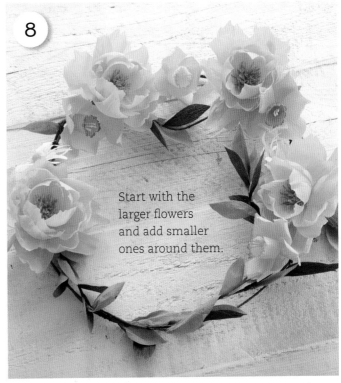

8 Start with the larger flowers and add smaller ones around them.

Boutonniere

For a wedding or other special event, boutonnieres add to the sense of occasion. If you make them from paper, you can prepare them well ahead of time and be sure they'll still look fresh on the big day.

You will need

- Paper flower
- Crepe paper
- 20-gauge florist wire
- Scissors
- Pencil
- Brush
- Pliers
- Ruler
- Pins
- Scrap surface
- Tracing paper
- Ribbon
- Spray mount
- Glue

1 Cut three leaves from green crepe paper and snip the edges to create a serrated effect.

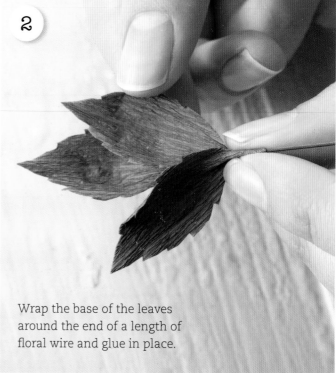

2 Wrap the base of the leaves around the end of a length of floral wire and glue in place.

3 Position the leaves at the base of the flower's head. Hold both wires together and wrap them with a long strip of green crepe paper.

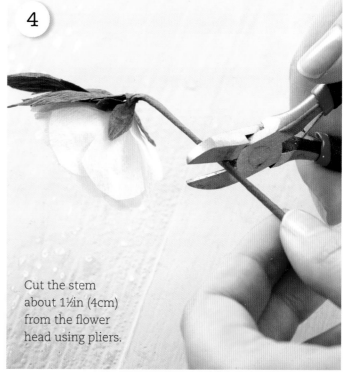

4 Cut the stem about 1½in (4cm) from the flower head using pliers.

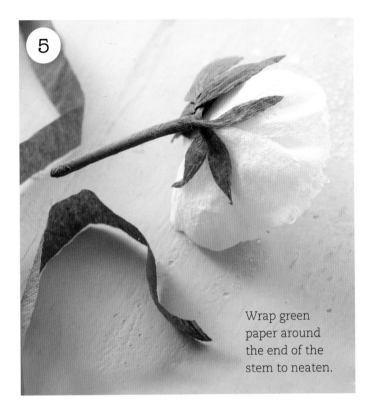

5

Wrap green paper around the end of the stem to neaten.

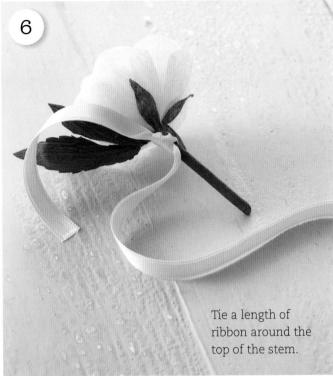

6

Tie a length of ribbon around the top of the stem.

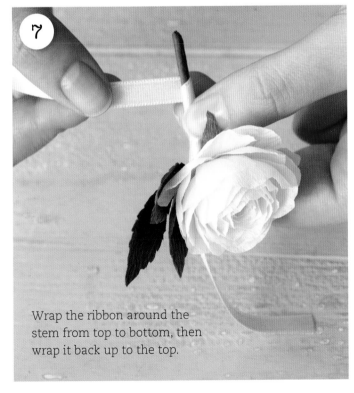

7

Wrap the ribbon around the stem from top to bottom, then wrap it back up to the top.

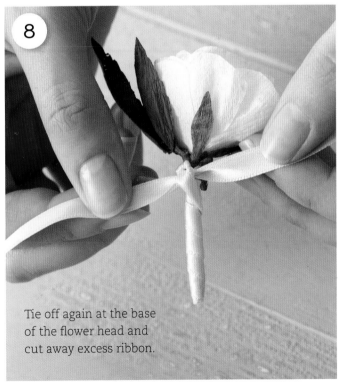

8

Tie off again at the base of the flower head and cut away excess ribbon.

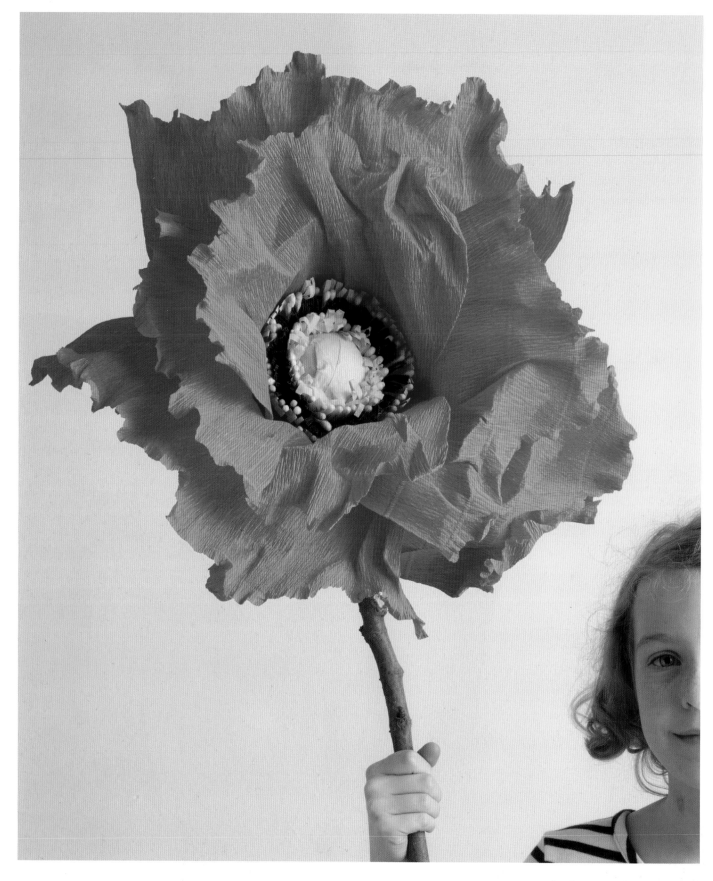

Large poppy

Guaranteed to make an impression, this giant poppy is
a real show stopper. It would make an excellent decoration
for a festival, party, child's room, or a wedding.

You will need

Crepe paper

Brush

Pencil

Scissors

2½in (6cm)
Polystyrene ball

Napkin

Glue gun and
glue stick

Scrap
surface

Acrylic paints

Cotton
swabs

Wrap a napkin or square of beige tissue paper around the polystyrene ball so that it is completely covered. Use a glue gun to secure it in place.

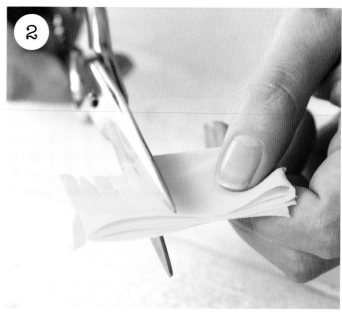

Cut a strip of yellow tissue paper slightly longer than the ball's circumference and 3in (8cm) wide. Fold it up and cut halfway into it from one side to create a fringed effect. Wrap around the ball and secure with the glue gun.

Mix your paint and slightly dilute it with water (you will need a mix of green and yellow buds). Dip the swabs in the paint to color them, then remove and set aside to dry.

Once dry, cut the yellow cotton swabs in half and stick them around the ball with a glue gun. Don't worry about making them perfect, you want them to look a little uneven.

5

Cut some black tissue paper as in Step 2, although this time it should be longer—in line with the wider circumference of the ball—and 4in (10cm) wide. Attach with hot glue.

6

The green cotton swabs for the stamens need to be a little longer, so instead of cutting them in half, cut the tips off of one end.

7

Glue the green buds around the outside of the ball so they fan out. You may find it easier to do this by attaching them lower on the ball.

8 Transfer the petal templates onto cardboard and cut them out. Draw around the templates onto the crepe paper, then cut out three small and three large petals.

9 Shape the top of the petals by twisting and stretching the paper. To achieve the petals' overall shape, work into the center of the petals with your thumbs to create curves.

10 Glue the small petals to the center of the flower, ensuring they are evenly spaced. Try to shape them to the curve of the ball as you stick them.

11 Shape the centers of the large petals in the same manner used for the small. Attach to the rest of the flower head, placing these petals in the gaps between the smaller petals.

12   Finally, carefully crumple the petals inward with your hands so that the ends curve into the center of the flower.

Festival headband

While primarily worn at festivals, these headbands have become increasingly popular at weddings and springtime events. Most combinations of bright flowers will work well.

You will need

Small peonies

Daffodils

20 and 26-gauge florist wire

Scrap surface

Pencil

Ruler

Tracing paper

Daisies

Large peonies

Scissors

Spray mount

Pliers

Glue

Crepe paper

1 Wrap two 14¼in (36cm) strips of 20-gauge wire in ⅝in (1.5cm) wide crepe paper, overlapping the ends of the wire by 3in (7.5cm).

2

Use crepe paper to secure the wires.

Measure your head with the wire, holding the point at which the two ends need to overlap. Glue in place.

3 Spray mount two shades of green crepe paper together. Cut out 25 leaves and pinch to shape.

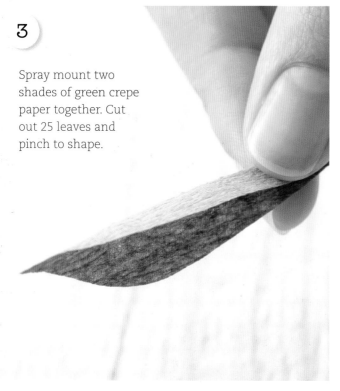

4 Make five stems with five leaves on each.

Wrap a 2½in (6cm) length of 20-gauge wire with a ⅝in (1.5cm) wide strip of crepe paper, tucking and gluing in the leaves between wraps.

5

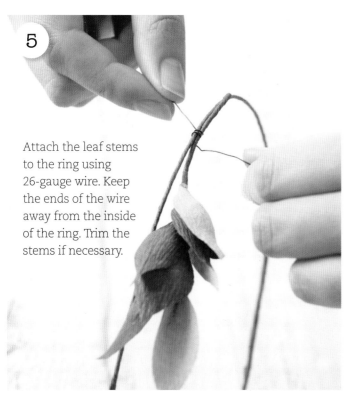

Attach the leaf stems to the ring using 26-gauge wire. Keep the ends of the wire away from the inside of the ring. Trim the stems if necessary.

6

Space the leaves out evenly, facing toward a focal point at the front of the ring. Leave a large gap at the back.

7

Attach the flowers using 26-gauge wire. Place a large peony at the focal point and space the other flowers around the headband.

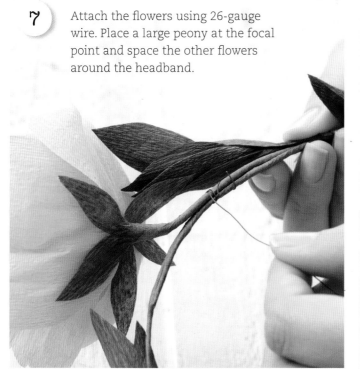

8

Wrap the ring of wire in strips of green crepe paper. This will cover up any bits of wire and strengthen the ring.

Scrapbooking

Edge punch

Paper

Making a scrapbook

Scrapbooks provide the perfect home for your photographs, letters, tickets, postcards, newspaper clippings, maps, gift tags, or anything else you find meaningful. The basic steps are simple: choose a theme and fill the book with mementos. After that it's just a matter of adding embellishments and decorations to make them your own.

The beauty of scrapbooks is that they feel truly personal to you. While popular themes include weddings, family history, travel, or a baby's first year, you can make them for just about anything you treasure.

The following pages cover some of the basic tools and know-how you'll need to get you started, but the secret to making the perfect scrapbook is simple—fill them with the things that mean the most to you.

Paper punch

Spiral-bound scrapbook or album

Glue dot
applicator

Foam pads

Paper tape

Bone folder

Assorted
cardstock

Edging
scissors

Patterned envelope

Photo corners and frames

Make your favorite photos look even more special by adding corners and frames. These steps can be adapted to fit photos of any size in your collection.

Photo corners

1 Cut a short strip of paper. Fold one leg at a right angle to the center.

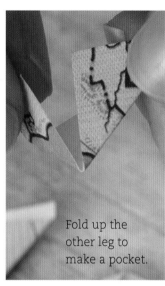

Fold up the other leg to make a pocket.

2 Trim any excess and slip a corner of your photo into each pocket. Tape to secure.

Retro photo frames

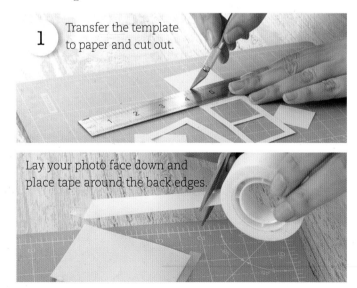

1 Transfer the template to paper and cut out.

Lay your photo face down and place tape around the back edges.

2 Turn the photo right side up and lay the frame over top.

Bunting and bows

If there is a lot of blank space left on your pages, try adding decorative elements such as bunting, ribbon, or these little paper bows. They can help to fill the space without making your pages look too cluttered.

Bunting

1 Fold a paper diamond in half and add double-sided tape.

Unpeel the tape's backing.

2 Close the diamond over a length of string to make the bunting.

Bows

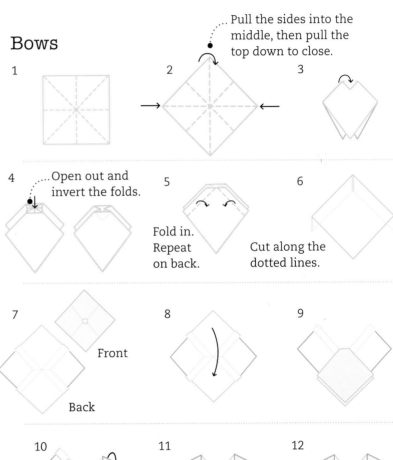

1

2 Pull the sides into the middle, then pull the top down to close.

3

4 Open out and invert the folds.

5 Fold in. Repeat on back.

6 Cut along the dotted lines.

7 Front / Back

8

9

10

11 Cut along dotted line.

12

13

14 Turn over and cut off the ends.

15 Fold into the middle.

Storage pockets

If you're looking to store items in your scrapbook without having to stick them directly onto the pages, create these storage pockets from paper. They're perfect for holding little mementos, and can be made in a range of shapes.

You will need

• Paper
• Scissors
• Glue or double-sided tape

Heart box

1   Turn the paper over.

2

3

4

5

6
7

8

9

10

11

12

Repeat steps 8–12 on the other side.

13

14

Envelopes

1
2

Apply glue or tape here.

3
4

Heart envelopes

1
2

3

4

Tuck into center.

Rosettes

Simple but eye-catching, rosettes are a great way to adorn your pages and add a little extra charm. The accordion fold used to make them can be used to make embellishments to a stroller or crib, but what you do with them is up to you.

You will need

- Paper
- Pencil
- Scorer
- Ruler
- Craft knife
- Double-sided tape
- Scrap surface
- Buttons
- Glue stick
- Edge punch
- Ribbon

Basic rosette

1 Draw and score a grid on a 3 x 8in (8 x 20cm) piece of paper.

Each section of the grid should be ½ x 1½in (1 x 4cm).

Cut the paper in half lengthwise, then fold each scored line like an accordion.

2

Attach the ends of the two lengths of folded paper with double-sided tape to form a circle.

Pram stroller

1 Cut out a ¾in (2cm) circle from cardstock and attach an accordion fold with double-sided tape.

Create wheels by sticking buttons to cardstock. Frill a piece of paper with an edge punch and glue across the middle of the circle as shown.

2

Tie a short piece of ribbon into a bow and stick it on for an extra flourish.

Gilding and embossing

Add an extra dimension to your embellishments by gilding or embossing them. We've gilded a doily and embossed a heart, but these techniques are easily adaptable.

Gilding

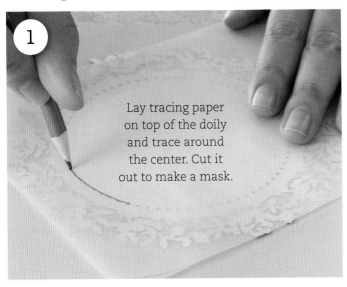

1 Lay tracing paper on top of the doily and trace around the center. Cut it out to make a mask.

2 Tape the mask to the doily and spray everything gold. Remove the mask and discard.

Embossing

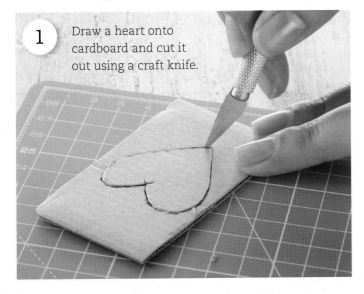

1 Draw a heart onto cardboard and cut it out using a craft knife.

2 Tape paper over the hole in the cardboard. Push a bone folder into the paper to emboss.

Travel

Use old maps to make envelopes or storage pockets.

Airmail envelope

Postage tags are a great way to incorporate handwritten notes.

Retrace your route with
string and paper stars.

Use a combination of frames and
photo corners to enhance your images.

Wedding

Edged frame

Embossed hearts

Gilding is a simple embellishment that's very effective.

Store confetti as a keepsake.

Heart box

Try making envelopes from different materials.

Baby's first year

Paper bunting

Paper bow

Retro photo frame

Edged frame

Glue on buttons as decorations.

Rosettes

Make miniature papercuts and put them in front of colored paper.

Templates

These templates can save you
time when putting together your
scrapbook. Scale them up or down
to suit your needs.

Retro photo frames
(pages 178–179)

Fold along the
dotted lines.

Baby bunting
(pages 180–181)

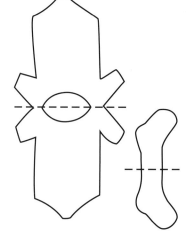

Heart envelope
(pages 182–183)

Envelope (page 191)

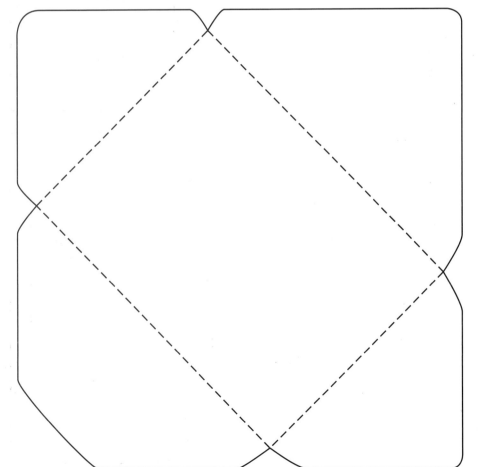

Bunting
(pages 180–181)

Envelope
(pages 182–183)

Templates

Pop-up bouquet (pages 14–19)

Enlarge to 145%

Score along dotted lines

Leaf x 1

Edge x 2

x 6

x 1

Central flowers x 4

Pink central flower x 1

x 3

x 2

x 2

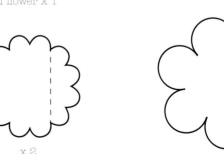

x 2

Feather gift tag (pages 20–23)

Enlarge to 125%

Score along
dotted lines

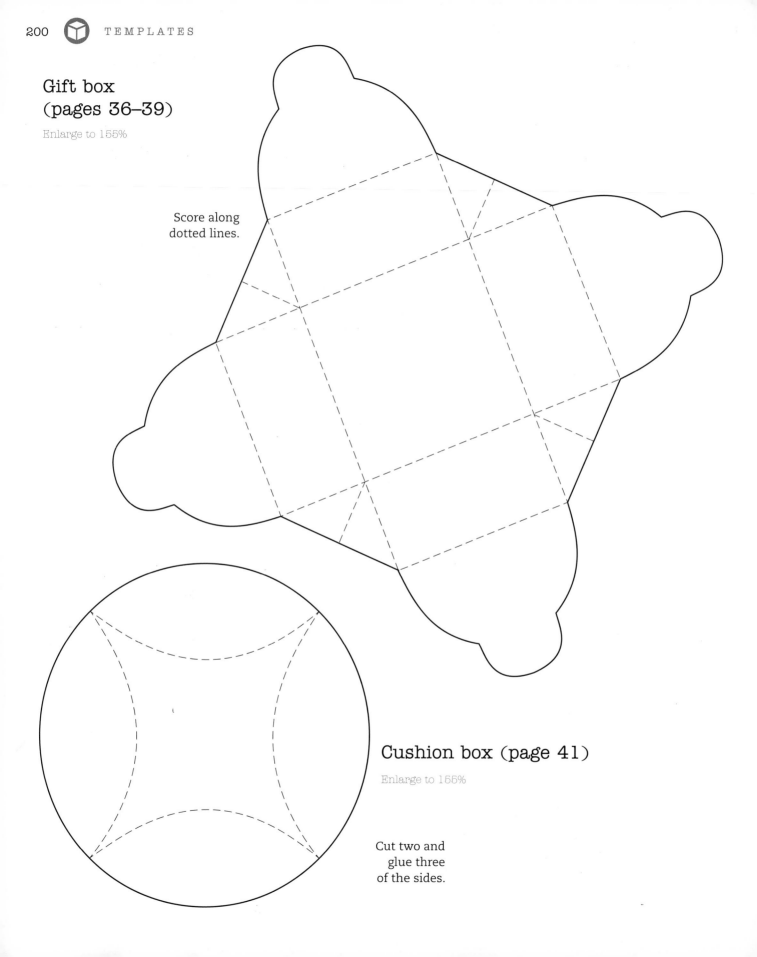

Gift box
(pages 36–39)

Enlarge to 155%

Score along
dotted lines.

Cushion box (page 41)

Enlarge to 155%

Cut two and
glue three
of the sides.

Pillow box (page 40)

Enlarge to 155%

3D star (pages 46–47)

Enlarge to 155%

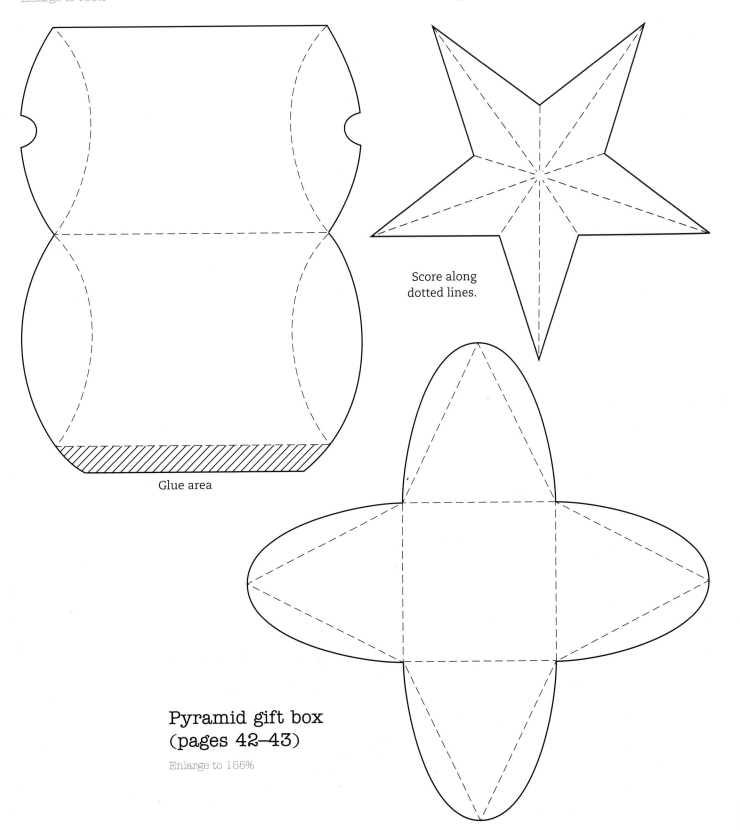

Glue area

Score along
dotted lines.

Pyramid gift box
(pages 42–43)

Enlarge to 155%

Layered papercut (pages 50–53)

Enlarge to 330%

Gray border (optional)

Lilac

Yellow

Pink

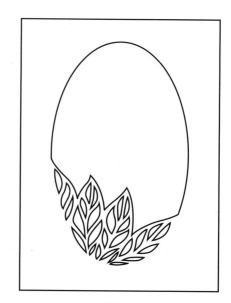

White

Papercut variation (page 54)

Enlarge to 330%

Gray border

Pastel pink

Teal

Orange

White

Oval papercut variation (page 55)

Enlarge to 330%

Gray border

Teal

Pastel pink

Orange

White

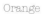

Nursery papercut (pages 60–63)

Actual size

Snowflake ornament (pages 98–101)

Scale to fit the size of the ornament

Papercut locket (pages 64–65)

Scale to fit the size of the locket

Papercut lantern
(pages 66–69)

Enlarge to 120%

Koi carp lantern (pages 70–71)

Enlarge to 165%

Lily lantern (pages 70–71)

Enlarge to 200%

Bear mask (pages 108–111)

Actual size

Scale band to fit.

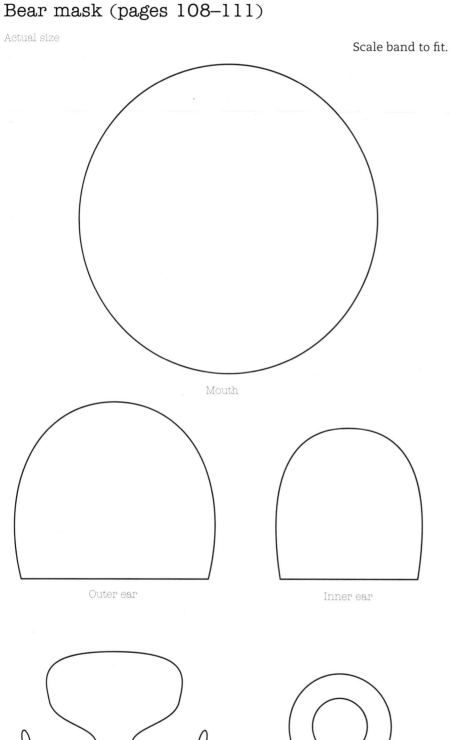

Mouth

Outer ear

Inner ear

Nose
(bear and dog)

Eye x 2
(bear and dog)

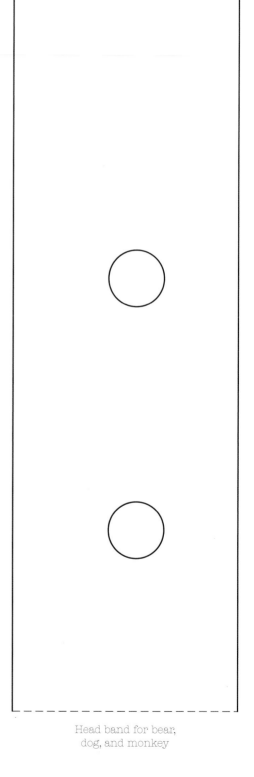

Head band for bear,
dog, and monkey

Dog mask (page 108)

Enlarge to 125%

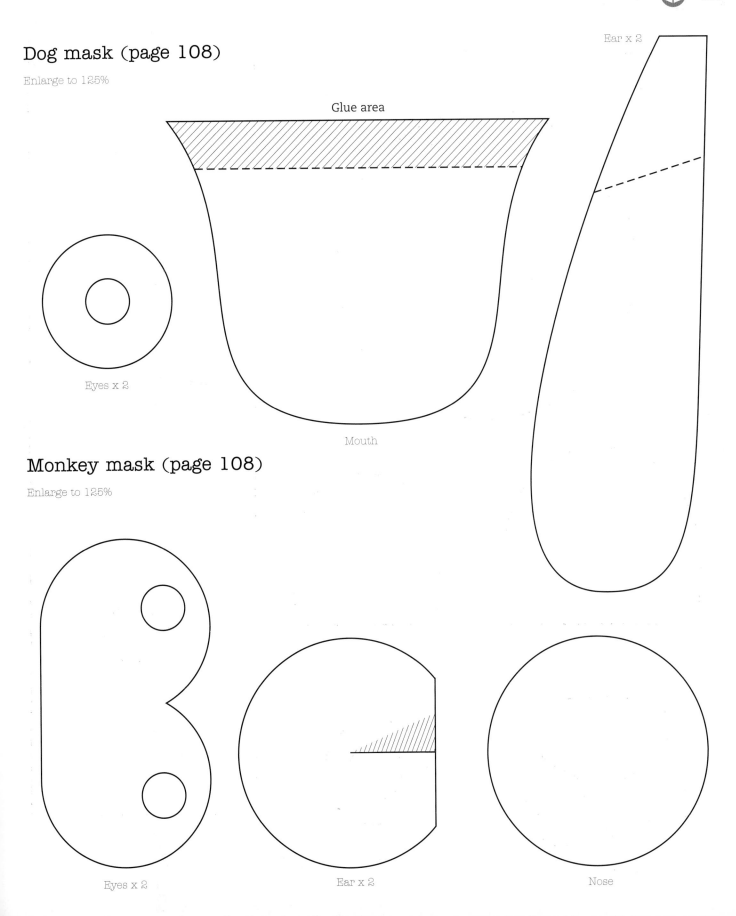

Glue area

Eyes x 2

Mouth

Ear x 2

Monkey mask (page 108)

Enlarge to 125%

Eyes x 2

Ear x 2

Nose

Nursery mobile (pages 112–117)

Actual size. Makes one owl.

Leaf x 4

Wing x 4

Score along
dotted lines.

Breast x 2

Eyes x 4

x 6

Body x 2

x 5

x 6

Party crown
(pages 118–121)

Enlarge to 125%

Scale band to fit.

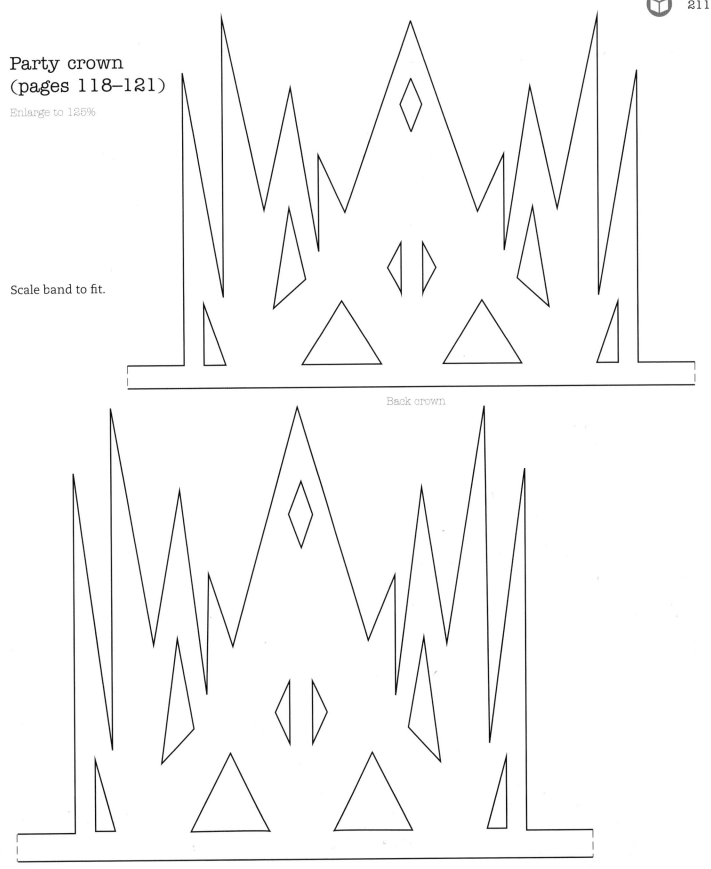

Back crown

Front crown

Butterfly crown (page 118)

Enlarge to 125%

Scale band to fit.

Headdress (page 118)

Enlarge to 120%

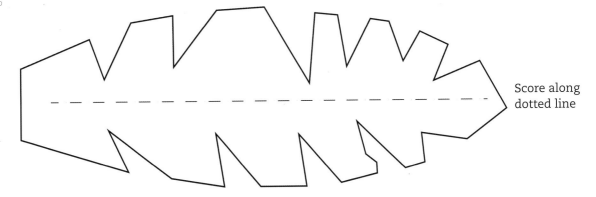

Score along
dotted line

Scale band to fit.

Star crown (page 118)

Enlarge to 120%

Scale band to fit.

Cherry blossom (pages 124–127)

Actual size

Lines show the direction of the grain.

Ranunculus (pages 132–135)

Actual size

Peony (pages 128–131)

Actual size

Small petal

Large petal

Leaves

Daisy (pages 136–139)

Actual size

Anemone (pages 140–143)

Actual size

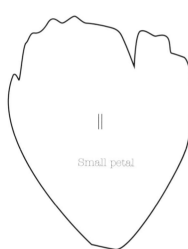

Petal

Leaves

Daffodil (pages 144–147)

Actual size

Petals

Place dotted line on fold of paper.

Trumpet

Daffodil leaves

Large rose (pages 148–151)

Enlarge to 155%

Small petal x 8

Large petal x 6

Sepals x 8

Large rose
(pages 148–151)

Enlarge to 155%

Medium petal x 10

Boutonniere
(pages 160–163)

Actual size

Lines indicate
the direction
of the grain.

Large leaf x 1

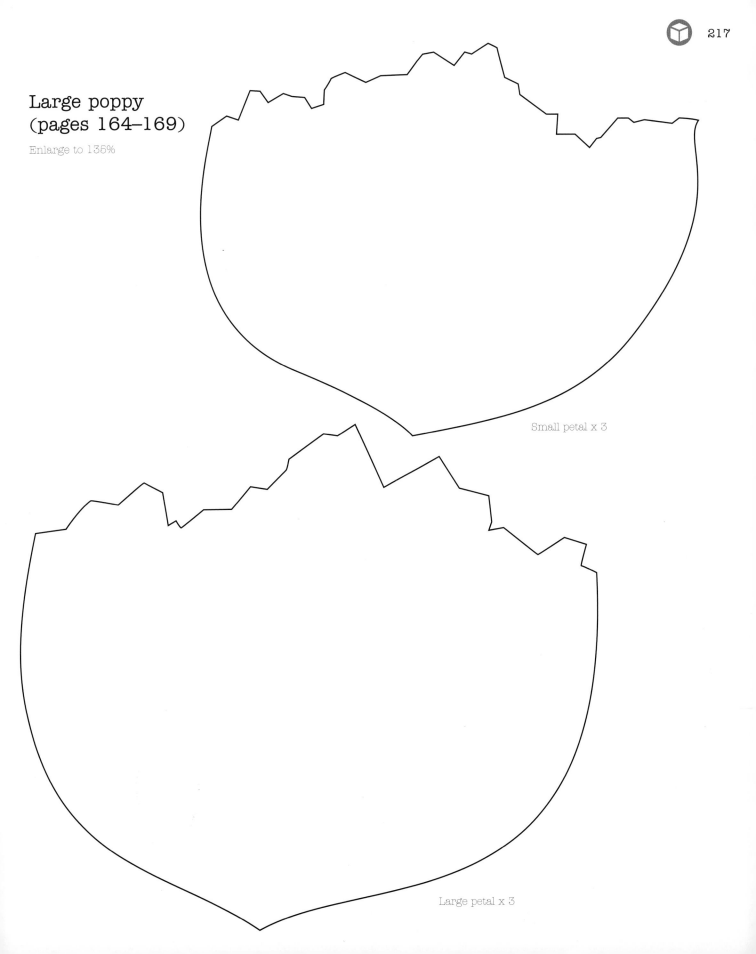

Large poppy
(pages 164–169)

Enlarge to 135%

Small petal x 3

Large petal x 3

Index

3D star tag 46–47, 201

Anemone 140–143
Animal mask 108–111, 208–209

Baby's first year scrapbook 192–193
bone folder 9
Boutonniere 160–163
Bows 180–181
brushes 9
Bunting 180–181

cards
    DIY envelopes 24–27
    Pop-up bouquet 14–19, 194
    Quilled 32–35
Cherry blossom 124–127, 214
circle punch 8
craft knife 8
crepe paper 11
Customized paper 44–45
cutting mat 8

Daffodil 144–147, 214
Daisy 136–139, 214
decorations
    Hanging fan 88–93
    Hanging garlands 94–97
    Honeycomb pom-pom 78–83
    Origami fairy lights 84–87
    Snowflake ornament 98–101, 205
DIY envelopes 24–27

embossing 186–187
equipment 8–9
eraser 9

fairy lights 84–87
fans 88–93
Feather gift tag 20–23, 199
Festival headband 170–173

flowers
    Anemone 140–143
    Boutonniere 160–163
    Cherry blossom 124–127, 214
    Daffodil 144–147, 214
    Daisy 136–139, 214
    Festival headband 170–173
    Kusudama 152–155
    Large Poppy 164–169, 217
    Large Rose 148–151, 215–216
    Peony 128–131, 214
    Ranunculus 132–135, 214
    Wreath 156–159

garlands 94–97
gift box: 36–41, 200–201
    Mini gift box 28–31
    Pyramid gift box 42–43, 201
gift tags
    3D star tag 46–47, 201
    Feather gift tag 20–23, 199
gift wrap: Customized paper 44–45
gifts
    Layered papercut 50–55, 202–204
    Nursery papercut 60–63, 205
    Papercut lantern 66–71, 206–207
    Papercut locket 64–65, 205
    Quilled earrings 56–59
    Silhouette frame 72–75
gilding 186–187
glue dots 9
glue sticks 9

Hanging fan 88–93
Hanging garlands 94–97
headband 170–173
hole punch 8
Honeycomb pom-pom 78–83
hot glue gun 9
jewelry
    Papercut locket 64–65,   205

Quilled earrings 56–59

kids' crafts
    Animal mask 108–111, 208–209
    Origami bird 104–107
    Owl mobile 112–117, 210
    Party crown 118–121, 211–213
Kusudama 152–155

lanterns 66–71
Large Poppy 164–169, 217
Large Rose 148–151, 215–216
Layered papercut 50–55, 202–204

masks 108–111
Mini gift box 28–31
mobile 112–117

Nursery papercut 60–63, 205

Origami bird 104–107
Origami fairy lights 84–87
Origami flowers 152–155
origami paper 11
ornaments 98–101
Owl mobile 112–117, 210

paper 10–11
    cardstock 11
    colors 10
    crepe paper 11
    origami paper 11
    quilling paper 11
    tissue paper 11
    tracing paper 11
    weight 10
papercuts
    Layered papercut 50–55, 202–204
    Nursery papercut 60–63, 205
    Papercut lantern 66–71, 206–207
    Papercut locket 64–65, 205

Party crown 118–121, 211–213
pencils, colored 9
pens 9
Peony 128–131, 214
Photo corners and frames 178–179
pliers 8
pom-poms 78–83
Pop-up bouquet 14–19, 198
poppies 164–169
PVA glue 9
Pyramid gift box 42–43, 201

quilling: 32–35
    Quilled earrings 56–59
    quilling paper 11
    shapes 34–35
    technique 34–35

Ranunculus 132–135, 214
roses 148–151
Rosettes 184–185

scissors 8
scorer 9
scrapbooking
    Baby's first year 192–193
    Bunting and bows 180–181
    equipment 177
    Gilding and embossing 186–187
    making a scrapbook 176
    Photo corners and frames
        178–179
    Rosettes 184–185
    Storage pockets 182–183
    Travel scrapbook 188–189
    Wedding scrapbook 190–191
Silhouette frame 72–75
Snowflake ornament 98–101, 205
spray mount 9
stamps 45
sticky tack 9

Storage pockets 182–183

tapes 9
templates 194–217
tissue paper 11
tracing paper 11
Travel scrapbook 188–189

utility knife 8

watercolor paints 9
Wedding scrapbook 190–191
Wreath 156–159

Acknowledgments

The creative team would like to thank the following crafters
for their hard work and expertise. We hope you are as inspired
by their talent as we are.

Sophie Pelham

Pop-up
bouquet

Nursery
mobile

Motoko Sugawara

Origami fairy
lights

Rochelle Falconer

Layered
papercut

Square
papercut

Oval
papercut

Bryony Fripp

Feather gift
tags

Gift boxes

Pillow boxes

Square boxes

Pyramid
boxes

Sonia Moore

Customized
paper

3D star tag

Origami birds

Bear mask

Monkey
mask

Dog mask

Ria Holland

Quilled cards

Gary Evans

Quilled
earrings

Katie Aldous

Large rose

Holly Owst

Large poppy

ACKNOWLEDGMENTS

223

Charlotte Bull

Photo corners and frames

Envelopes and pockets

Rosettes

Gilding and embossing

Travel scrapbook

Wedding scrapbook

Baby scrapbook

Susan Beech

Cherry blossom

Peony

Ranunculus

Daisy

Anemone

Daffodil

Wreath

Boutonniere

Festival headband

Danielle Gallagher

Papercut lanterns

Koi carp variation

Star crown

Floral crown

Spiky crown

Feather crown

Snowflake ornament

Emma Stevens

Nursery papercut

Papercut locket

Clare Shedden

Honeycomb pom-pom

Martine Charalambou

Silhouette frames

Hanging garlands

Hanging fan

DK would also like to thank

Marie Lorimer for preparing the index. Claire Cordier and Lucy Claxton for picture library assistance. Andy Crawford for photographing the pom-pom project. Paperchase for the loan of props for the fans project. Olive and Florence Pugsley, Aeden Jenkins, Carlow and Devon Day-Lewis, Tyler-Justin, Alighla and Isabella Gallagher for modeling. Tilly Lee, Danielle Glover, and Alice Bowsher for hand-modeling.